Musical
Instruments

Musical Instruments

ALAN KENDALL

HAMLYN

First published 1972 by
Hamlyn Publishing
Bridge House, London Road
Twickenham, Middlesex

© Copyright
The Hamlyn Publishing Group Limited 1972

Revised edition © Copyright 1985
The Hamlyn Publishing Group Limited

ISBN 0 600 50159 0

Printed in Portugal

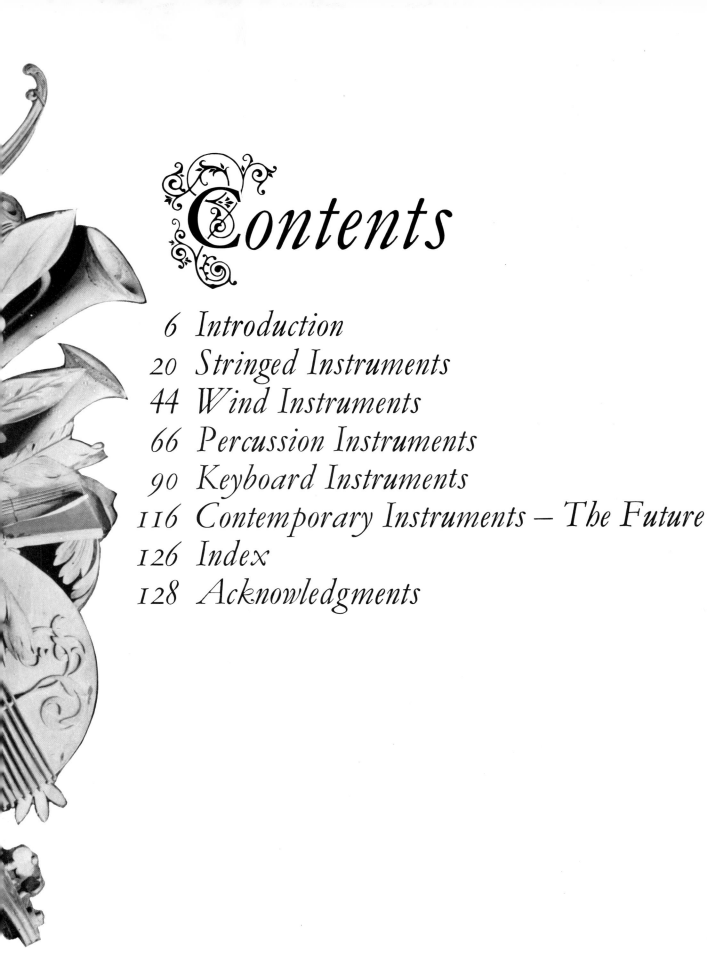

Contents

Introduction

Below: angel musicians from the right-hand of three organ shutters by Hans Memling in the Koninklijk Museum voor Schone Kunsten in Antwerp. The fiddle at right has pegs secured in the vertical plane and the angel bows with the hand on the under side of the bow. The extremely thick keys of the portative organ are played with one hand, whilst the angel activates the bellows with the other.

Anyone, however small or rudimentary his knowledge of music, who looks at a group of instrumentalists – preferably an orchestra – playing together, can see at once that some of the instruments have strings and are being played with a bow or plucked with the fingers; others are being blown and others struck, and some played from a keyboard. In this book we have deliberately adopted this very basic classification or way of grouping musical instruments – strings, wind, percussion and keyboard – because it is easier for a person who is not a trained musician to relate what he hears to what he sees, rather than take on trust something technical he does not understand. Naturally this is a very empirical approach and is far too simple. As we shall see later on in the book, the grouping of keyboard instruments, for example, includes wind (organ), strings (piano) and percussion (glockenspiel), but because the playing technique which unites them is a more readily identifiable characteristic than their actual method of producing sound, they fit together best in this group.

Various other classifications have been proposed, and the one which probably makes most sense from a technical point of view is that which divides instruments into four groupings. These are the idiophones or all the percussion instruments apart from drums or any other instruments which produce their sound from a vibrating membrane; the chordophones or stringed instruments; the membranophones or instruments which produce their sound from a vibrating membrane and the aerophones or instruments which have vibrating air as their main source of sound. By this token both the organ, with a little thought, and the oboe are visibly aerophones, but is the piano easily recognizable as a chordophone? Ordinary people, and certainly the instrumentalists themselves, rarely think of instruments in this way. They see them as something much more concrete, as part of a continuous process of evolution that stretches back into antiquity and is still going on. However, the evolution of musical instruments is not necessarily a process of continuing progress. Some instruments are at an arrested stage of development, whilst others are in a state of decline, such as the guitar in its electrified state.

The intention of this book is to describe the chief classical musical instruments of the Western world; how they differ from each other and from some of their chief counterparts in the rest of the world; also how they came to be what they are today and their relationships with some of the world's

Top: the central portion of the decoration over the top of the title page of Michael Praetorius' *Syntagma Musicum* of 1615–20, which was an encyclopedic work on music, and had a section devoted entirely to instruments, which were being used increasingly in Lutheran Churches. Through his book, Praetorius gave added impetus to the practice. Here we see a group of wind players and the conductor to the right of the organist.

Bottom: a group of monks representing the five orders playing, from left to right, a rebec-type instrument, a psaltery, what is apparently a transverse flute, a lute, a recorder and, in the foreground, a harp, from a manuscript in the British Museum. In the Middle Ages the Church had increasingly to come to terms with secular music, and often popular songs were used as themes for masses.

Opposite top: music has always been used in both East and West to add dignity to ceremonial and state occasions. In this drawing, based on an Indian painting, both large and small kettledrums are seen, played with rather thin sticks, as well as cymbals and shawms played in the position known as *en chamade*. In the background are wind instruments similar to cornetts.

Opposite bottom: the familiar stance of musicians has always inspired painting and sculpture, and the elegant costume of the 18th century was particularly suited to these German wood carvings of a flautist and a violinist in the Victoria and Albert Museum, London. The somewhat fanciful sloping shoulders of the violin may have a slight relation to some local form or tradition.

9

Opposite top: an angel concert by Paolo Veneziano in the Palazzo Venezia, Rome, including a tambourine, a shawm, what is possibly a cittern, a mandora, two portative organs, a fiddle and two psalteries.

Opposite bottom: the left shutter of the Memling group (see illustration pp. 6–7). Note the plectra of the angel playing the psaltery; the Gothic tracery of the tromba marina soundhole, and the singing lutenist angel.

Above: a Garden of Love from a manuscript in the Biblioteca Estense, Modena. The *hortus conclusus* or enclosed garden sprang from the Garden of Eden, but here is totally secularised.

11

folk instruments. In other words, how the main types of instruments developed over the centuries, and the basic principles by which they function.

The remarkable thing about musical instruments is that the moment one begins to look at them one is taken beyond the purely technical domain. For one thing they have been intimately bound up with man's history since time immemorial, and are therefore an integral part of it. The persistence of association in this context is remarkably strong. To take a very current example, since the evolution of the pop group, in itself an interesting phenomenon in sociological terms, the guitar has seen an immense revival. Its apotheosis, in some people's eyes, is the electric guitar, which is played as if it were a classical guitar although even this convention is being abandoned, and in some groups the guitarists now hold their instruments upright in front of them, either standing or seated, rather as viols are held. From a purely typological point of view, however, the electric guitar has absolutely nothing to do with the guitar proper any more. Yet we continue to think of it as a guitar, and it retains a surrealistic approximation to the shape of a guitar, as if it had sprouted horns or melted in the heat of performance. In point of fact, there is no reason for retaining this curious shape. The guitar soundbox has been virtually replaced by an amplifier, and the only remaining relevant part of the instrument is the fretted neck with the strings running along it. There is, however, a perfectly good explanation for this, which is by no means the same thing as justification. We want to think of this electric instrument as a guitar and the performer as possibly some kind of minstrel. The images we have of musical instruments are so strong that they are able to withstand potentially devastating onslaughts.

To take another example, the organ of a famous London church is electronic. The large console, or point from which it is played, is readily visible. The sound rings around the vaults, and to all intents and purposes one is listening to an instrument in the great tradition of church organs. What one hears, however, owes more to the cinema, with all due respect to the church in question. It is troubling not to be able to see any pipes, but that is presumably better than being able to see a loudspeaker suspended from the roof. Fake pipes would be worse still, and merely revert to the electric guitar syndrome. The Church, in her wisdom, eschews counterfeit and relies on the combination of majestic noise and beautiful architecture to distract the too inquisitive. Such is our confidence in our ability to know what is what, that we allow ourselves to be taken in or, to put it in a more kindly way, we all have some very basic concepts about musical instruments, often without realizing the fact. A few may be misguided; if so, we hope to illuminate some of the darker regions.

The trained musician may well be somewhat surprised to find little or no mention here of the question of pitch. For a person who has no conception of pitch beyond the fact that notes vary from high to low, it is extremely confusing to learn that, like truth seen in philosophical terms, it is a very relative thing. It has consequently been the policy not to involve added complications and therefore pitch has only been discussed when absolutely essential. It is a particularly vexed question when considering old musical instruments, and to go into it in any satisfactory way would require much more space than is available here. On the other hand, absence of details about pitch is no impediment to the appreciation of musical instruments themselves, nor need it impair the utility of a book such as this.

Because of the very important part music has played in men's lives, instruments of music have always been lovingly created and decorated, and artists have depicted them in their paintings. This has both advantages and disadvantages when it comes to considering illustrations of instruments for a book. Decoration and a beautiful finish may make an instrument extremely photogenic, but it is no guarantee of the instrument's innate musical qualities. Frequently musical instruments tend to be of better quality the more discreet and refined their decoration, though this is by no means a rule. One is therefore torn between showing a beautifully decorated spinet, for example, which is of little musical interest, or a visually dull spinet which is nevertheless of immense musical interest. Secondly, artists are not necessarily going to be musicians, and although they may well paint beautiful compositions of instruments, these are often shown in somewhat improbable combinations from a musical point of view. They may also paint the instruments in such a way that nothing of musical value can be learnt from the painting. A picture may contain what would seem to be a member of the violin family, but without indicating the number of strings, the shape of the soundholes or details of the bridge or tailpiece, the picture is of little or no value to the musician.

Some artists, however, were highly acute in their observation of the scene in front of them, and most faithful in reproducing it. As a result we have very useful information as to when the position of the pegs on the violin was altered or when the playing position of the lute was modified. As it happens, these two examples just cited are documented elsewhere, so the paintings merely serve as corroboration; but there have been instances of carvings or paintings giving vital clues to the musician. This is by no means an attempt to say that all art must be objectively realistic to the point of being merely photographic, but it has naturally been our endeavour to choose illustrations for their usefulness and accuracy and reject the merely pretty.

13

Above: The Sharp Family on the
Thames at Fulham, by Zoffany.
From left to right the instruments
are violin, 'cello, serpent, two
oboes, two horns and two
clarinets on top of a small
harpsichord, and theorbo, which
may already have been obsolete
by this time. There is, however, a
fine instrument by Michael
Rauche in the Victoria and
Albert Museum, made in London
in 1762 (see illustration p. 26).
The oboes, clarinets and horns
which are shown in this painting
have survived to the present.
Opposite top: Jan Breughel, The
Sense of Hearing, 1625, in the
Prado, Madrid. Allegory and
personification have always been
elements in the history of art,
from the gods and heroes of
classical antiquity to the sins and
virtues of the Middle Ages and
the conceits of Mannerist and

Baroque art. Here the sense of
hearing is shown only secondarily
as the product of people making
music, but relies on the
association of the sounds made by
the instruments.
Opposite bottom: chamber music
has sustained and extended the
talents of both composers and
instrumentalists, and in the
opinion of some musicians distils
the essential essence of music.
Today the basic form of the
chamber ensemble is the string
quartet, with its parallel
development in the wind section.
Here Ben Shahn's Quartet, 1944,
from a private collection in New
Jersey, has the traditional violin
and 'cello, but the second violin
and viola are replaced by a guitar
and mouth organ.

At the same time we have attempted to show the large extent of the world of musical instruments, and that in effect it is almost as wide as man's own experience. The virtuoso player would doubtless regard his instrument as an extension of himself. Certainly the care and attention given to his instrument is equivalent to that lavished on a child—and not only when a musician possesses a Stradivarius violin, or because his violin is his means of earning his living—the wood and the glue, the gut and the resin are handled in such a way as to produce an entirely unique experience in the hands of its owner. There is a kind of alchemy which takes place, beyond technical and scientific methods of registering and processing data. Thomas Mace, writing in *Musick's Monument* in 1676, suggests that the lute, being a sensitive instrument, should be put '. . . into Bed, that is constantly used, between the Rug and Blanket; . . . only to be excepted, That no Person be so inconsiderate, as to Tumble down upon the Bed whilst the Lute is There; for I have known several Good Lutes spoil'd with such a Trick'. One would be even more reluctant to put a violin to bed in this case, but modern players will take no less care of their instruments.

In an age in which everyone is clamouring to speak and very few people are prepared to listen, musicians, through their instruments, have a marvellous opportunity for communication. People do, and will, listen to music. It is one of the means of communication that is truly international, for it embraces not only all nationalities, but all levels of appreciation and accomplishments—the young starting out to play and making his first agonizing notes just as much as the confident concert performer he may well one day aspire to be. We must do all that we can to encourage interest, not in any starry-eyed way, for music can be one of the most cruel of disciplines, but in a full realization of what is likely to be involved. If this book in any way helps to further interest in music, then it will amply reward our efforts.

Opposite left: Pandean Minstrels in Performance at Vauxhall. Panpipes had long disappeared in the West – except as a folk instrument in some countries – when they were re-introduced as a novelty in the 18th century to form a band, along with cymbals, triangle, drum, Turkish Crescent and tambourine with jingles.

Opposite top: a 19th-century photograph of Persian musicians. Two sizes of kettledrum – rather on Indian lines – are seen, both played with thin sticks, and two vastly differing sizes of wind instrument. The playing position of the kneeling figure in the right foreground is very different from that employed in the West today.

Opposite bottom: the inscription on the chamber organ means: 'Let everything that hath breath praise the Lord'. In addition to the strings and brass instruments, hanging on the wall are horns, triangle with jingles, cornetts, and what is possibly a large cittern. Note that the conductor directs with rolled-up music.

Below: a photograph of 1884 showing a group of London street musicians playing, from left to right, harp with pedals, violin, cornet and three-stringed double bass. Although presumably itinerant, this can hardly have been a very mobile combination. Such bands have not entirely disappeared from central London, even today.

Two very interesting aspects of music making in 18th-century Germany. The large illustration is Adolf Menzel's *Flute Concert in Sans Souci*, the palace built by Frederick II of Prussia. The king was himself an accomplished performer on the flute, and was taught by Joachim Quantz. It was as a result of his visit to Potsdam in 1747 that Bach wrote his *Musical Offering*. The smaller picture shows a Collegium Musicum of about 1775 from a family album in the Germanisches National Museum, Nuremberg. The performers stand around the harpsichord, with the accompanist in the foreground with his back to the viewer.

Stringed Instruments

In the view of many people the string quartet is one of the finest achievements of Western Classical music, which has remained unaltered since its creation in the 18th century. There had been forerunners in the consorts of the 16th and 17th centuries, but it was only in the hands of Mozart, Haydn and Beethoven that the string quartet became the medium in which the four performers – first and second violins, viola and cello – met together as equals, exploring and developing the material in a seemingly endless variety of ways. In the late Beethoven quartets, as the deaf composer retreated more and more into his inner world, one becomes aware that one is being invited to share his most profound musical thoughts, and in the twentieth century, the string quartets distilled some of Bartók's most intense musical language. Seen here is the Melos Quartet.

The basic principle of all stringed instruments is that a length of gut, wire, silk or nylon held in tension between two points is made to vibrate, and it is the vibration of the string – whether plucked, struck or bowed – which emits the sound or note. However, the sound is hardly audible unless a soundboard or box is provided to amplify it, and it is the transmission of the vibrations of the strings to the soundboard which gives the different stringed instruments their many varied timbres. Keyboard stringed instruments, apart from the hurdy gurdy, have deliberately been excluded from this section, and are dealt with in Chapter 5, but this is a useful point at which to bear in mind that the term strings is today used in a very narrow sense to denote the members of the violin family. Just how many different instruments do belong to this category will be seen shortly. First, however, some general considerations about stringed instruments.

The importance of the soundboard or box in connection with the strings has already been mentioned, and the different ways in which the strings relate to the soundbox provide three main categories of stringed instrument. First there are the instruments in which the strings pass across the soundbox, which has a neck attached to it, and the strings are stopped or shortened along the neck to give the different notes. Violins and lutes are examples of this group, as well as the ancient lyre, despite the fact that lyre strings were not stopped against a fingerboard. The second category of stringed instrument has no projecting neck to the soundbox and examples are the zither and dulcimer. The third category, of which the harp is the sole representative, has a projecting arm at an angle, and the strings pass from the arm to the soundbox, forming the familiar triangular shape of the instrument. No one of these three groups is especially older than the others. Harps and lyres, for example, have been found together in tombs excavated in Mesopotamia, and in wall carvings and mosaic decorations from that area.

In the first category the soundbox is generally in two parts. The box itself is usually of a fairly hard wood, and the lid or soundboard, which is glued to it, is of a softer wood. This, however, is a very basic generalization, because the soundbox of a lute is made up of a number of separate strips of wood which are put together and shaped over a mould to give the familiar pear-shaped effect. In a guitar the bottom of the box is flat, but the sides, like those of a violin, are extremely curved, and to achieve this effect they are moulded to the

Vier kleine Geigen one bünde/vñ mit dreien Seyten

Discantus.

Altus.

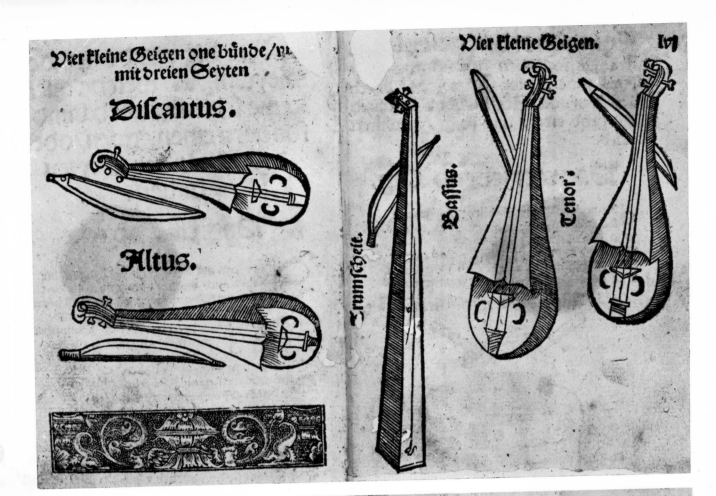

Trommscheit.

Baſſus.

Tenor.

Das zehend Capitel.

So darff man der müh vnd arbeit gar nicht
Welche durch das abſetzen geſchicht.
Wer vorſtendig iſt/der mag es faſſen
Den groben knolln wirds nicht ſein zu maſſen.

Vier kleine Geigen mit bünden/vnd mit dreien Seyten.

Discantus.

Altus.

Tenor.

Baſſus.

Folget ein Tabelthur/aus den Noten inn die buchſtaben geſatzt/ Vnd dienet auff allerley einſtimmige Inſtrument.

22

desired shape on a hot pipe. Some old instruments were carved out of a single piece of wood, so that soundbox and soundboard were organically united, but if the instruments in question are later than about AD 1600 then they are almost certainly amateur work.

Nylon has been introduced extensively nowadays, but traditionally, the strings are of metal (steel or brass), sheep's gut or silk. The strings pass over a bridge which transfers the vibrations to the soundboard. In the lute and guitar the bridge is glued directly on to the soundboard and the strings are attached to it. In the violin family, however, and indeed in most bowed instruments, the strings are held taut over the bridge and attached to the bottom of the instrument by means of a tailpiece. At the upper end, the strings are tuned by increasing or decreasing the tension in them, thus raising or lowering the pitch. The idea of a standard pitch is a fairly recent one, and indeed there is still a good deal of variation in different parts of the world. It is something which has come with the advent of travel and mass communications and the introduction of standardized tuning. Previously, as long as a group of instrumentalists were in tune with each other, that was all that mattered.

Bows

The bow with which the strings are made to vibrate took its name from the weapon and it has undergone a long process of development which began in the thirteenth century. From that time until the eighteenth century bows were much more curved along the upper side, and therefore more like the weapon.

It was the Parisian François Tourte (1747–1835) who really gave the modern bow its form and made the business of bow-making into a science. Before him a state of anarchy may be said to have prevailed, not only in the making of bows, but also in their use. Composers rarely bothered to give indications as to how a piece was to be played by the strings, whereas nowadays considerable effort is devoted to showing what a composer has in mind.

The use of the bow can make a series of notes sound *legato* by slow, even pressure and no breaks in the stream of sound, or *staccato* by playing virtually each note with a new, short stroke and so breaking the flow of sound. Occasionally a composer will indicate that the wood, or upper part of the bow, is to be used on the string, thus effectively turning the bow upside down and giving a hollow sound.

Unlike the bowstring of the weapon, a musician's bow has hair which he can tighten and release with a screw mechanism at the bottom end, where it is held in the hand. To make better contact with the strings of the instrument, or to get more grip, he coats the hair with rosin in block form. This is what a string player is usually doing when he seems to be warming up his bow before playing.

The way in which the bow is held makes a considerable difference to the quality of tone produced. The most striking contrast is seen when comparing a viol player who holds his bow with his hand under the end of it and a violinist who

Opposite: Martin Agricola's *Musica Instrumentalis Deutsch*, published in 1528, has several inaccuracies, and owed much to Sebastian Virdung's *Musica getutscht* of 1511. Of the two families of instruments shown here, the upper one is most accurate, and shows a set of rebecs with the addition of a trumscheit or tromba marina. The lower set of fiddle-like

instruments is more fanciful. *Below:* a silver lyre from Ur, now reconstructed, in the British Museum. It dates from about 2,600 BC and is 106 cms high. The instrument was tuned by the sticks or levers along the top bar. This was a refinement of the simpler and possibly earlier method of tuning, which was to wind all the strings round the bar, which was then turned.

holds his bow with his hand on top of the end. The latter can exert more pressure and get a more incisive quality into his playing, whereas the viol player has little or no attack.

Most orchestras use bowing patterns which are generally decided between the conductor and the leader of the orchestra, who is always the first violin, and the leaders of the other sections. One notable exception among conductors was Leopold Stokowski, who encouraged his players to use whatever bowing suited them best.

The way in which the player puts his fingers on the strings gives variety to the tonal quality. If he moves his fingers back and forth, a *vibrato* or ringing effect is obtained. When he plucks the strings with his bowing hand fingers, a *pizzicato* or clipped effect is the result.

The fingerboard runs along the neck, under the strings, and in some instruments there are marks called frets to show the player where to stop the strings to produce the semitones. Viols and lutes have pieces of gut knotted around the neck to produce frets, whereas guitars–certainly the later ones–have brass or silver frets let into the neck. These refinements took place over many centuries, however, and in particular in the centuries after the period known in Europe as the Middle Ages.

Lyres

The lyre, possibly the oldest stringed instrument, was traditionally invented by the Greek god Hermes, or Mercury as known to the Romans. He is said to have taken the shell of a tortoise and some cow gut to make the first lyre. But in fact we have to go further back in time than pre-Classical Greece, to Ur in Mesopotamia in the third millennium BC, for the appearance and development of this instrument. Two types seem to have existed then; a small instrument with four or five strings which had a ritual function, and a larger, eleven-stringed variety used for secular purposes, as shown in the banquet scene on the Standard of Ur in the British Museum. The lyre at this time was played with the fingers alone and without the plectrum as in later years. In Egypt under the New Kingdom, lyres were played with the plectrum, but they never became really popular instruments in that country. King David's harp was in all probability not a harp at all, but a lyre which he used to brighten the gloom of Saul's madness. It was the same instrument which the Jews refused to play when they were exiled in Babylon, but hung on the willow trees.

The lyre came into its own in Greece, and is most associated with pre-Classical antiquity. In fact, as the attribute of the god Apollo, to whom it was given by Hermes, it can be said to have represented the higher side of the Greek character—moderation, balance and control, intelligence and taste—against the Dionysian, orgiastic (and, by implication, foreign) drunkenness of the pipes. The famous contest between Apollo and Marsyas, in which Apollo played the lyre and Marsyas the flute, was a direct confrontation in these terms. There were two forms of lyre current; the heavy, solid instrument with a wooden soundboard which was used to accompany the narration of epics, and the smaller version with two arms projecting from the round body, which was either a tortoise shell or a wooden bowl covered with skin to provide resonance. A horizontal bar ran between the two arms to carry the strings, which were attached at the base of the body and held away from it by a bridge. The traditional number of strings was seven, though in fact they varied from three to twelve.

The lyre survived in Northern Europe as the rote, and during the Middle Ages people began to play it with a fiddle bow. Later survivals were the bowed lyre in Finland and Estonia, and the crwth in Wales. The last authentic specimens of the crwth date from the eighteenth century and have bass strings which lie along the side of the neck. These were not stopped and bowed, but struck open, either with the thumb or the bow. There was a deliberate revival of the lyre when neo-Classicism was all the rage at the end of the eighteenth century and beginning of the nineteenth. These instruments are highly decorative and some of them certainly look very much like their classical counterparts. Technically, however, many of them are more akin to the guitar than the lyre.

Lutes

The earliest pictorial representation of a lute, which is the forerunner of most of our modern stringed instruments, and in particular the violin family, dates from the late third millennium BC, and the sound-producing principle must therefore have been known before that date if people were able to represent it so clearly. As in the lyre, the strings of the lute are stretched across the soundbox, but they then pass

along a neck, against which they are stopped to raise the pitch, with one hand, whilst the other hand strikes them over the sound-box. It is a curious paradox that the harps and lyres of Mesopotamia were regarded as much more refined at the time, and that the lute was a barbarian instrument which emanated from the mountain tribes to the north east. The lute has not survived in its ancient form in the Near East, but we can see from illustrations that the soundbox was small and oval in shape, the neck long and thin and the strings—of which there were only two or three—plucked with a plectrum. It was introduced into Egypt, however, and as a result has survived in a somewhat debased version in North Africa.

The lute was never taken up by the Greeks and Romans, though curiously it next appeared—as a short lute—in an area of North West India strongly influenced by Greece. The lute was also taken to China and Japan. In China, under the Han Dynasty (206 BC–AD 220), the short lute flourished as p'i-p'a, and subsequently in Japan as biwa. In India the lute developed in its broadnecked form as the sitar with its many variants. In renewing interest in Indian music and its instruments, Western Europeans have simply retraced the path of development of Islamic influence in the East. In the West, at a somewhat later date, Islam brought, amongst other things, the lute to Europe.

The lute arrived in Europe in the thirteenth century during

the Crusades. During the fifteenth and sixteenth centuries it became immensely important, and its popularity lasted into the eighteenth century. It became Europeanized during the course of the fourteenth century, and the Arab style of playing with a plectrum was abandoned in favour of the fingers, and playing several parts or 'voices' at once. Naturally, the tone produced was softer than when played with a plectrum. Eventually the playing position altered too. If one looks at Piero della Francesca's *Nativity* in the National Gallery, London, one sees that the two angels playing lutes hold them across their chests. This is not the artist's fancy. Lutes were played in this position at the time, and the seated position with the instrument across the knees is a subsequent development. Paintings can be of help in such matters, but they can also be misleading, and one has to be wary.

In the sixteenth century the lute was made of sycamore, cypress or sandalwood and the belly was of pine, with a carved rose soundhole. Often the tension in the strings would cause the belly to buckle or warp and to counteract this it could have been reinforced inside with struts glued across the under surface of the belly. The neck of the lute has seven to ten gut frets or markers to show the player where to put his fingers, and the top is bent back at a right angle. Decoration is kept to a minimum to keep weight down, and not spoil the equilibrium of the instrument. In the sixteenth century there was an

Above centre: a drawing by Jacopo Bertoja in the Uffizi, Florence. The string player points to the music whilst the lutenist tunes. The flautist in the background either warms up his instrument, if proceedings have not begun, or else practises the passage over which they may have come to grief.

Above: three members of the lute family: (1) an arch lute with its split head, (2) a mandoline with four strings of double courses, and (3) a mandola with six single-course strings. The exact distinction between the arch lute and the theorbo is confused, if in fact any distinction exists at all.

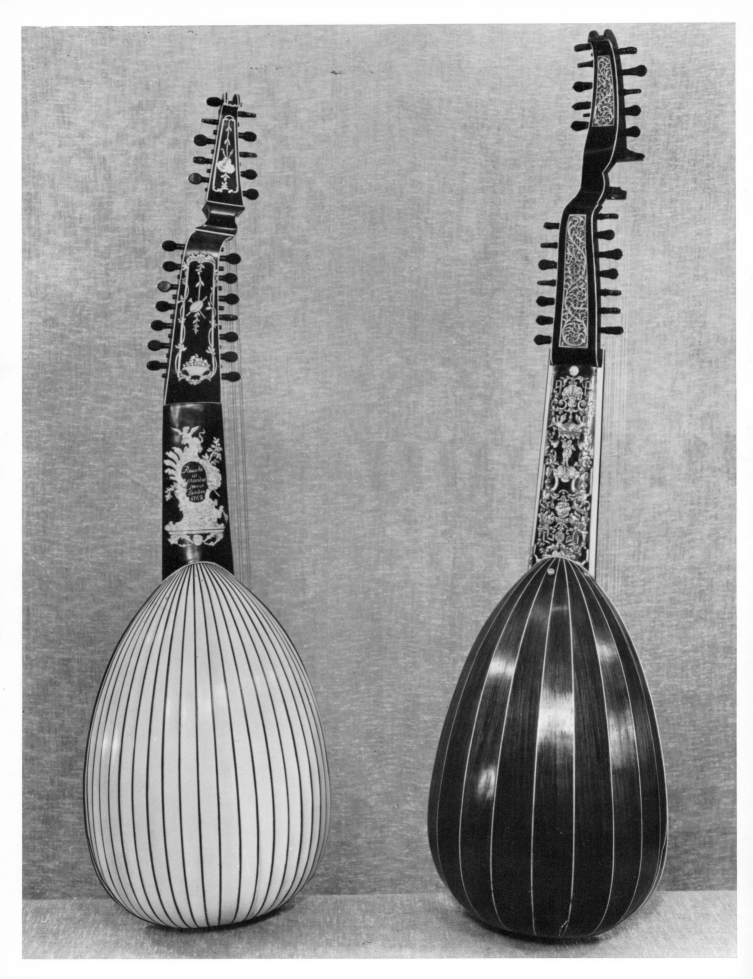

interest in increasing the downward compass of instruments generally, and the lute was affected by this trend. More bass strings were added, thereby increasing the original six to eleven. This made it virtually impossible for the player to reach all of them to stop them, and as a result the theorbo–lute was born. Basically the idea was to split the head into two; one part bent back as before, the other a straight continuation of the neck, so that the deeper strings could be given greater length. Without this greater length a much thicker gut would have been necessary, which would have been both clumsy and difficult to tune satisfactorily. Overspun strings – that is gut strings bound with fine metal wire – had not been developed as yet.

A distinction should be made between the theorbo and the theorbo-lute. Basically the theorbo has a double head, but instead of the main course part of the head being bent back, it follows straight up, and the bass part is above it, thus making a much longer neck and head altogether. Initially the theorbo seems to have had single strings or courses, but in the seventeenth century they were double, or a mixture of double and single. At this time the instrument was used a great deal with the bass viol as a continuo or accompaniment instrument, whereas the lute was a solo instrument. Theorbos are also known as arch-lutes, but some sources restrict this term to the chitarrone, which has a smaller body, longer neck, and is sometimes strung entirely in metal, which obviously gives a much more brilliant sound.

There are various folk lutes which have survived, such as the cobsa of Romania and Moldavia; a Russian theorbo known as torban and a Ukranian lute. Sweden also produced its own lute, or more exactly theorbo.

Mandolins and long lutes

Mandolins are virtually small lutes, and for most people recall Italy, and Naples in particular. There was an earlier version known as a mandore, which had a long history and was very popular in the twelfth and thirteenth centuries with jongleurs. Both the mandore and mandolin were intended as melodic instruments and the distinction between them lies mainly in the strings. Usually the mandolin has four pairs of strings tuned rather like a violin, and mandores have gut strings attached to the bridge rather on the lines of a guitar, whereas the mandolin has some or all of its strings of metal, and they are attached to the base of the instrument. The mandolin is played with a plectrum generally, whereas the mandore was usually plucked with the fingers only – though not exclusively. Mandores have gut frets, whereas mandolins have metal or ivory.

The term long lutes includes a variety of folk instruments such as the Arab buzuk, the Turkish saz, the Greek bouzouki and the Yugoslav tamboritsa, which have small bodies with round backs, long necks, and are played with a plectrum. They are also wire strung. There was a Western version known as a colascione, but this is now obsolete. The triangular Russian balalaika is a modification of an older instrument, the domra, and is often regarded as a member of this family.

Opposite: two theorboes from the collection of the Victoria and Albert Museum. The one on the left was made by Michael Rauche in London in 1762, and that on the right by J. H. Goldt in Hamburg in 1734.
Left: a terracotta plaque, now in the British Museum, which comes from Babylonia and dates from the early part of the second millennium BC. It is 7.5 cms high and shows a man wearing a kilt and playing a long-necked lute.

Citterns

The cittern is closely related to the lute, though in appearance has much in common with the guitar family, which will be considered next. Citterns are fretted and metal strung, as are some mandolins and guitars, but citterns owed a great deal of their popularity to this fact at one time, because metal strings make for bright tone, as we have seen with the chitarrone and mandolin, and also stay in tune much longer than a gut-strung instrument. Another feature of metal strings is that they break less easily. The replacement rate is thus much lower, and the likelihood of physical discomfort less, as anyone who has been hit by a snapping 'cello string will appreciate. Citterns generally have a flat back and belly and straight sides, and a somewhat pear-shaped silhouette. The strings are attached at the bottom of the instrument. In profile the cittern is very like a violin, and it is no surprise, therefore, to learn that both the great violin-makers Gasparo da Salò and Stradivari also made citterns.

Two instruments which may be mentioned here are the pandore or bandora, and the orpharion. The first was said to have been invented by the great English viol-maker John Rose. Unfortunately no known specimen of the instrument survives, though there is an orpharion by Rose which is in the collection of Lord Tollemache at Helmingham Hall in Suffolk. A much more popular development of the cittern in England, however, was the instrument which became known as the English guitar. The use of the word guitar is very confusing because it is not a guitar at all, and the word guittern, much more similar to cittern, would be more apt. The English guitar was not in fact a specifically English product, and was also very popular in France. It was essentially a drawing-room instrument on which well-bred young ladies might exhibit their talents, and was often highly and richly ornamented.

A North German version of the cittern was the bell cittern, with the outline of a bell, as the name implies. Portugal had its own version which originally may have influenced all the rest. Spain had the bandurria, which might be strung with gut or metal. There was also a fair amount of cittern-making practised in Scandinavia, so that one gets the impression of a very fluid situation, in which it is difficult to be too dogmatic about origins and influences.

"JUST RUN YOUR EYE ALONG DESE STRINGS"

Guitars

It seems possible that the guitar was introduced into Spain by the Arabs from the East. There are twelfth-century illustrations which show instruments similar to what we now know as guitars. However, it would be unwise to say that the guitar had an unbroken line of development from some Near Eastern ancestors. Certainly by the middle of the sixteenth century the guitar was very popular in France, and later in Italy and Spain itself. Then at the end of the eighteenth century and the beginning of the nineteenth it spread across the whole of Europe, and enjoyed a popularity unrivalled until our own century.

The early guitars had only four strings, often double courses or with the first single and the rest double. When the instrument became popular at the end of the eighteenth century a new form of stringing was adopted. Six single strings replaced the four courses – traditionally three of gut and three of overspun silk – though metal stringing was also not uncommon. It is one of the curious gaps in musical historical knowledge that no one knows exactly when or where the four-string guitar became a six-string instrument. However, in the first half of the nineteenth century several refinements in guitar-making were introduced, and from places as far apart as Naples and New York.

In addition to experiments to improve the sonority and musical quality of the guitar there were purely mechanical experiments to improve the technique. Keys were introduced, though more specifically for the cittern than the guitar, and a system copied from the pedals of the harp known as ditals. The fact that they failed to establish themselves as permanent features of the instrument is ample evidence of their merely transitory nature.

Before leaving the guitar family, mention must be made of two of its most popular members, the ukulele, which had Portuguese antecedents, and the banjo, which has a vellum or parchment belly stretched over a hoop, and no back. It may have gone to America with slaves from Africa, and therefore, like so many instruments of this group, could possibly have had Arab origins. Whatever the truth of the matter, it was certainly well established in the New World in the seventeenth and eighteenth centuries, and from there came back to the Old World. Its origins and popularity in the last century are vividly shown in a piece of advertising in the author's possession called *Banjo Praises* which proudly announces that it may be sung ANYWHERE without permission. A minstrel is holding what must have been a very heavy banjo, had it ever existed, and when the page is held horizontally the curious organization of the strings reveals the name of a popular patent medicine. A far cry from the divine strains of Orpheus!

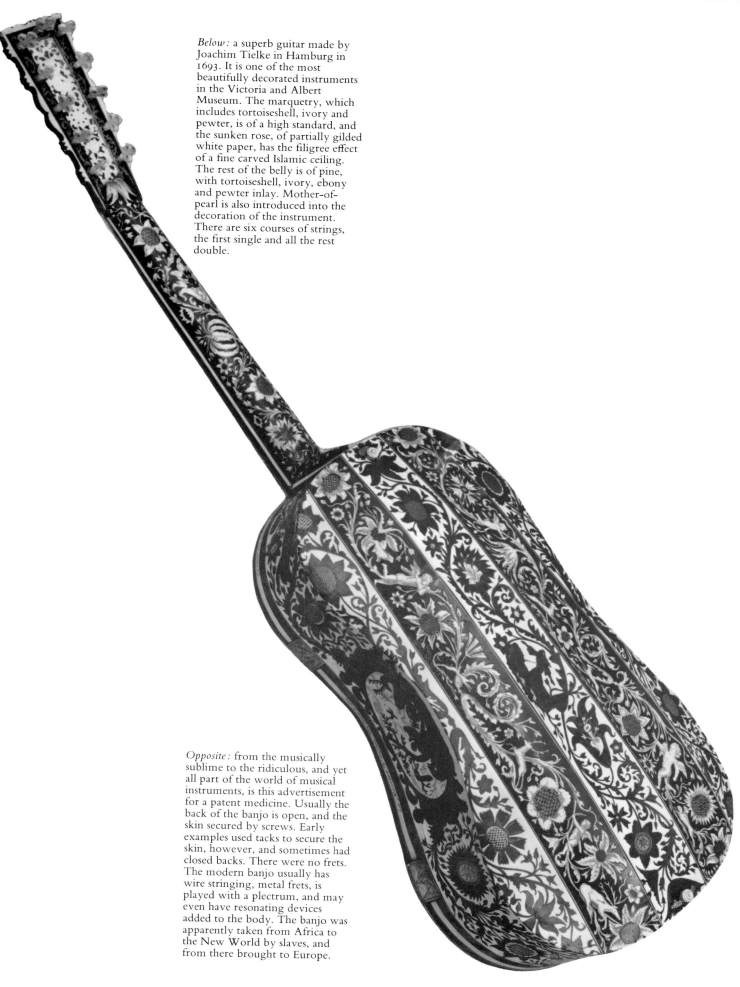

Below: a superb guitar made by Joachim Tielke in Hamburg in 1693. It is one of the most beautifully decorated instruments in the Victoria and Albert Museum. The marquetry, which includes tortoiseshell, ivory and pewter, is of a high standard, and the sunken rose, of partially gilded white paper, has the filigree effect of a fine carved Islamic ceiling. The rest of the belly is of pine, with tortoiseshell, ivory, ebony and pewter inlay. Mother-of-pearl is also introduced into the decoration of the instrument. There are six courses of strings, the first single and all the rest double.

Opposite: from the musically sublime to the ridiculous, and yet all part of the world of musical instruments, is this advertisement for a patent medicine. Usually the back of the banjo is open, and the skin secured by screws. Early examples used tacks to secure the skin, however, and sometimes had closed backs. There were no frets. The modern banjo usually has wire stringing, metal frets, is played with a plectrum, and may even have resonating devices added to the body. The banjo was apparently taken from Africa to the New World by slaves, and from there brought to Europe.

109

THE VIOLIN FAMILY

The exact origin of the word fiddle and the instrument itself are still surrounded with a great deal of uncertainty. There are Spanish manuscript illuminations of bowed instruments dating from the tenth and eleventh centuries, but the first representation of a violin as such is in a fresco by Gaudenzio Ferrari which dates from about 1535 in Saronna Cathedral in Italy. In the intervening five hundred years there was a wide variety of instruments in existence.

One of the most clearly distinguishable forms to survive the Middle Ages, however, was the lira—obviously related to lyre. In practice it was known as a viola, and the fact that some of these instruments were later adapted for use as what we know as violas today shows that they were closely related to each other. This sort of cannibalism is, incidentally, a great problem when dealing with old instruments, for they were frequently adapted by later generations, and it is often difficult to decide what the original form of any one instrument was. As far as one can see, the lira da braccio (played at the shoulder) had five double courses on the fingerboard, and two bass courses. The pegs for tuning the strings were not inserted

laterally or in the side, as in later members of the violin family, but perpendicularly. There was also a larger variety, known as lira de gamba, played like a 'cello.

Another fiddle to survive from the Middle Ages was the rebec. Its long pear shape, with a round back and flat soundboard, looks distinctly medieval, and it was possibly of Byzantine origin. It continued to be made in France and Italy into the eighteenth century, though had already been replaced in the sixteenth century by the violin. It survives in Eastern Europe as a folk instrument—gadulka in Bulgaria, lyra in Greece and liritsa in Dalmatia, though this may have been a by-product of the later rebec by way of Italy.

The earliest known surviving violins date from about 1560, and are the work of Andrea Amati (born before 1511: died about 1580), of Cremona, and Gasparo da Salò (1540–1609) from near Brescia. Later came Andrea's grandson, Nicolò (1596–1684) and the famous Stradivari (born about 1642–1737) and Guarneri, under whose inspiration the form of the violin was perfected.

Most early violins had only three strings, in contrast to the modern four, and small violins were made both for children and, apparently, professional use, since Bach's First Brandenburg Concerto calls for a violino piccolo. One should not confuse the smaller violins with the kit, or dancing master's pocket violin, which was made to accompany dancing lessons indoors. Some have four sympathetic wire strings in addition to the four playing strings. The nature and function of sympathetic strings is dealt with on p. 32, under viola d'amore.

Next to the violin in size is the viola. Until the end of the seventeenth century it was made in two sizes, since orchestral music had two middle parts below the second violin up to that time. As the violoncello developed it tended to take over the role of the second viola, and decreased in size. In fact originally the 'cello played the bass of the orchestra, and might have either four or five strings. Now, of course, four is the accepted number. One notices a similar situation with old double basses, though there the number of strings might by anything from four to six. Some of these date from the later sixteenth century, showing a large variety of features, so that in many respects the double bass is the least standardized member of the modern violin family. In recent years there has been a tendency to increase the length of the lowest string, taking it up to the tip of the scroll. This effectively gives the double bass an extra four notes, which are controlled by an attachment with keys. The keys can be locked in position to give the string its normal sounding length, and when lower notes are required, may be quickly unlocked with a flick of the thumb. This arrangement is particularly useful in playing Bach where the double basses double the 'cellos at the octave below. With the extra lower notes they are able to play in unbroken phrases, and do not have to jump up an octave when their part goes below G.

Viols

There is a tendency to think of viols as violins that were

30

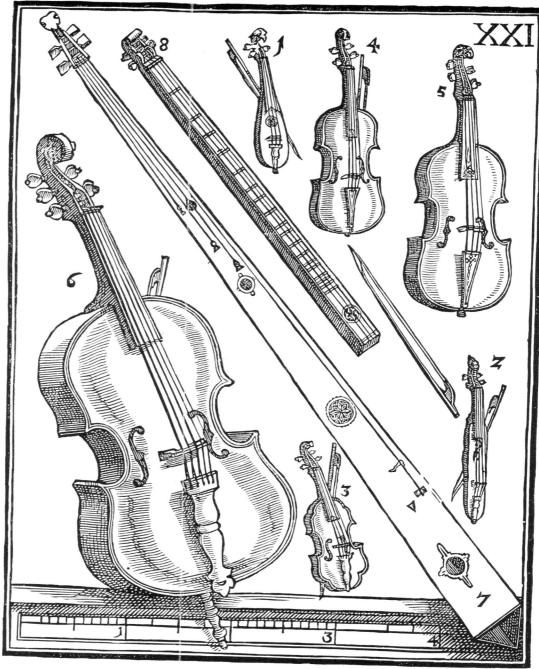

A group of stringed instruments comprising plate XXI of Michael Praetorius' *Syntagma Musicum* (see illustration p. 8).

somehow neglected in the march of instrumental progress. This is far from the truth, because both the viol and the violin emerged in their separate forms at the same time – the middle of the sixteenth century – and initially the viol was the more popular instrument, with a much more extensive repertoire. Apart from the actual sound, the chief feature which distinguishes viols from violins is the way in which they are played. The body of the viol is held downwards, on the lap or between the knees – hence the Italian term viola da gamba. There are illustrations showing this playing position from the twelfth century, but it is difficult to say very much about the instruments themselves, and it is not until the later fifteenth century that there is clear documentation for the viol in terms of its subsequent identity. There are generally six gut strings, which give a softer timbre by comparison with the overspun strings of the violin family. The frets on the fingerboard are

also of gut. The main field of interest for the viol was the consort, one of the forerunners of the string quartet, and for the bass viol the role of continuo instrument. In recent times it has been revived for the accompanying of recitatives in an attempt to give a more authentic account of certain works.

This is an appropriate point at which to consider the evolution of the string quartet. Nowadays we tend to think of chamber music as an entity in itself, and the string quartet in particular as the distillation of its very essence. In the late Beethoven quartets, for example, the intensity of the musical experience and of the sentiments expressed is, for many people, one of the summits of classical music.

It is easy to make the visual and intellectual jump back in time to the viol consorts of the late sixteenth and early seventeenth centuries and to see that here was the beginning of a tradition. However, although for once something in the history of instruments and their music seems simple, this unfortunately is far from being the case. True, there was an early tradition of consort playing which in England survived late into the seventeenth century in the string music of Purcell. But that music must be seen as the close of an earlier age, and not the dawn of a new one.

In fact it is Haydn who is usually credited with the invention of the string quartet, but as the great scholar Marion Scott put it: 'Haydn did not invent the form: he made it—an infinitely higher achievement.' This is not to attempt to say that there was nothing written for strings alone in between Purcell and Haydn, a space of almost forty years. In Italy there was Tartini and the brothers Sammartini; in Mannheim there were such composers as Johann Stamitz and Franz Xaver Richter, and in Vienna Florian Gassmann.

However, much of this music was simply music for strings which remained orchestral in conception, and was virtually a symphony for string orchestra which the conductor directed from the harpsichord. Often the first and second violins, instead of being individual voices or parts, are scored in unison and are therefore treated in a very orchestral way. The viola is used to fill in the harmony, except when playing in fugal passages, and the 'cello is treated very much as part of the bass-line and harpsichord continuo. This is obviously a very different concept from that of the members of the string quartet as solo voices, as they have now become established.

The strings were also treated in another way in the period between Purcell and Haydn, particularly by the Mannheim School. In the compositions of Richter and Johann Stamitz all the parts are of equal importance. No one instrument is inferior or relegated to an accompanying role. They are all solo instruments. This is the key to their real nature, for they are more akin to the small or *concertante* group of players set off against the larger group, or *ripieno*, in the *concerti grossi*. It may have been that some composers saw in these *concertante* groups the beginnings of the string quartet. If we look at Haydn's earliest excursions into the medium, however, we see at once where for him in particular the idea sprang from.

One summer—possibly somewhere round about 1755, when Haydn was twenty-two or -three years old—a Viennese nobleman called Count Fürnberg invited a group of string players to his country home for a musical evening. Haydn was to write the music as well as join in its performance. There would be no harpsichord continuo, only strings, so Haydn wrote a series of *divertimenti*, and this is how he described the first string quartets. In this way he ceased to rely on the harpsichord to put the filling into the musical cake, but learned how to write for the strings alone in such a way that they were solely responsible for bringing harmonic richness to the whole. It soon became apparent that strings treated in this way could sound quite as well as, if not better than, strings accompanied by the incessant plangent tones of the harpsichord.

One can see, then, that although consorts of viols were in a way forerunners of string quartets, the progression was neither direct nor unbroken. There was considerable over-lapping—at both ends of the timescale.

The early Italian violin makers—such as Amati and Gasparo de Salò—also made viols, though in the late sixteenth and early seventeenth centuries it was the English who led the field in viol-making. Towards the end of the seventeenth century, however, France, Germany and the Low Countries seized the initiative, and in France in particular there was quite a revival of interest which lasted until well into the eighteenth century. It is probably this revival which was responsible for the pardessus de viole and the quinton, the former a version of the treble viol, and the latter a five-stringed instrument to be played at the shoulder.

The viola d'amore must be given a special mention here, because of the sympathetic wires. These wires lie under the fingerboard and vibrate in sympathy with the playing strings. The pegs for these wires, which are also used on some Asiatic instruments, such as the Indian sitar, are generally above those for the bowed or playing strings. The viola d'amore is played at the shoulder and has no frets. The effect of the sympathetic wires sounding 'in sympathy' with the bowed strings is particularly delicate, like a silvery echo, and although the

repertoire for the instrument is small, it is used to telling effect in Bach's *St John Passion*. After the scourging of Christ has been announced brilliantly and brutally by the tenor Evangelist, the bass then has a quiet, intimate aria of contemplation, the accompaniment of which is scored for two viole d'amore and lute. The effect is that of a soothing lullaby after the physical horror of the scourging.

Before leaving the viol family, mention should be made of the baryton, which is an elaboration of the bass viol with sympathetic wires. However, on the baryton the wires are arranged in such a way that they can be struck with the thumb. Generally there were no frets, but there is an example in the Royal College of Music, London, with seven gut frets. Haydn wrote several Divertimenti for baryton for Prince Nicolas Esterhazy, his patron.

Two other instruments which were sometimes given sympathetic wires can be conveniently mentioned at this point. The first is the tromba marina or trumpet marine. Its shape is quite unique, as if the bell of some huge wooden trombone had been placed vertically on the ground. Normally it had only one string of gut, though there are known specimens with two. One of the two feet of the bridge was left free to vibrate, and a bow was used, but in addition the string was touched, so that it gave the harmonics also. The sympathetic wires were an optional addition, and no doubt welcome in an instrument of such limited resources. When a string is stopped, the player presses hard with his finger against the fingerboard, and the vibrating length of the string is shortened, thus altering the pitch of the note. With harmonics, however, he only lightly touches a point (known as a nodal point) on the string, and thus achieves an overtone. It is of course possible to have a harmonic for a stopped string by touching the portion between the fingerboard and the bridge for a very high note. Harmonics are not exclusive to strings, they are also obtained by wind, but there, and this is particularly true of the brass section, they are regularly used to form the scale, whereas in strings, harmonics are an additional effect.

Last of the instruments which have sympathetic wires is the hurdy gurdy. The strings are of gut, and they are sounded by a rosined wheel which is turned inside the instrument. The

Below left: a Stradivarius violin in the Museo Civico at Cremona. Antonio Stradivari, who was probably born in 1644 and died in Cremona in 1737, can be said to have brought the violin to perfection. He coincided with the great Italian school of violin playing, of which Corelli was the greatest exponent. Stradivari's work was mainly concerned with the lower arched belly and increasing the size of the bouts or sharp curves cut out of the sides of the violin. Some five or six hundred of his instruments – not all violins – have survived, though he probably made twice this number.

Below: this illumination from the Manesseh Codex in Heidelberg University Library shows Heinrich von Meissen (otherwise known as Frauenlob) with some of his pupils. He founded the first school of Meistersingers, and seen here is a variety of instruments, including a tabor and recorder, a shawm, two five-stringed fiddles, a psaltery and a set of bagpipes. The Meistersingers were similar to the troubadours of France, except that they were less well-born. By a social comparison the Minnesingers were more on a par with the French troubadours, and preceded the Meistersingers by some two hundred years.

Opposite top: a musical gathering in 18th-century Italy as portrayed by the artist Gabbiani. The painting is in the Pitti Palace, Florence. The four upper strings – two violins and two violas – are bowed 'over-arm', whereas the gamba is bowed 'under-arm'. The two other players have a mandoline or some similar instrument, and a single-manual harpsichord, whose keys are white with black accidentals. There is quite an attempt at realism here, particularly in the varying thickness in the 'cello strings, for example, and the way in which the players look at the spectator is particularly effective.

Opposite bottom: this *Still-life with Musical Instruments* by Pieter Claesz, 1597/8–1661 is especially interesting when compared with the illustration of the same instruments on p. 31. Here the artist has made a fairly accurate attempt at reproducing the instruments as he sees them, but avoids any means of suggesting their sound capabilities. He rather takes pleasure in them simply as shapes and colours, the result of man's skill in manipulating wood and glue and the tools of his craft. The instruments are 'cello, violin and lute, and hanging up in the background are a flute and a cornett.

The hurdy-gurdy enjoyed aristocratic favour in 18th-century France. This instrument belonged to Adélaïde, Madame de France, the third daughter of Louis XV, and is made of lemon-tree and box wood. It has a fringe of mother-of-pearl medallions and is inlaid with tourquoises. The illustration below shows a fashionable lady of the period playing her hurdy-gurdy.

Opposite: an Egyptian painting of the Sait period. The harp has a fine head finial on its post, but there would appear to be ten pegs and only nine strings.

earliest depictions are found in manuscripts dating from the twelfth century. The strings are stopped by wooden keys, operated with the left hand, and the wheel is turned by the right hand. The hurdy gurdy is mainly a folk instrument, though in France it had a period of glory when it was taken up by the aristocracy in the reign of Louis XIV. It still survives in France, though it has reverted to its folk role. Some of the strings act as drones, which make the hurdy gurdy a string counterpart to the bagpipes. The loose bridge is a feature in common with the tromba marina. There are some bowed hurdy gurdies (i.e. without a wheel), and some with a wheel and no keys, so that the stopping is done with the fingers directly. From this it was a short step to the organ hurdy gurdy, and most people would probably tend now to think of the hurdy gurdy first as an organ. The basic principle is the same, however, the keys acting as organ keys and the wheel operating the bellows.

Zithers, psalteries and dulcimers

The common feature of all these instruments is that they have no neck. However, whereas zithers and psalteries are plucked or bowed, the dulcimer is struck with sticks or hammers, and is therefore a forerunner of the piano. The difference between the zither and psaltery is that the zither has fretted strings and those of the psaltery are open. In the zither the strings are stretched over a body, which may or may not be the soundbox. Some of the eastern stick zithers have a gourd attached as a resonator. Tube zithers use a cylindrical portion of a tree, or in some cases half a section, and board zithers, as the term suggests, are flat. These zithers are of particular interest in relation to stringed keyboard instruments. Between the tube and board zithers are long zithers, which are associated especially with the Far East, and in China the long zither is traditionally regarded as the oldest stringed instrument.

Features common to all Chinese zithers are the convex board and silk strings, which are more penetrating than those of gut, but less shrill than metal. The shê is unfretted, with twenty-five open strings. There is a smaller version known as a cheng, or so-no-koto in Japanese. Extensive use of harmonics is made when playing the ch'in, with a great deal of glissando (sliding effect) and vibrato. The effect, as one can imagine, is exotic and Kurt Sachs, in his monumental work *The History of Musical Instruments* (now sadly in need of revision), gives this description of it:

'Occidental listeners have great difficulty in perceiving the delicate shades of ch'in playing and in appreciating its spirituality. But the average Oriental cannot appreciate it either. The ch'in does not court popularity, nor does it suit dilettantism. It is the instrument of philosophers and sages. In the privacy of a closed room, alone or before a few selected friends who listen respectfully and silently, the immaterial notes of the ch'in reveal to the listeners the ultimate truths of life and religion.'

Apparently zithers were not known in Assyria and Egypt, but they were in Phoenicia and Israel, as the Psalms testify. One of the oldest and longest surviving medieval zithers was the monochord. As the name implies, it had a single string over a soundbox and was plucked or bowed. It had much in common with the tromba marina, even to the extent of occasionally having sympathetic wires. The zither associated with South Germany, Austria, and part of Switzerland is probably a descendant of the monochord. Some of the strings are open, and give the effect of a drone, as in the hurdy gurdy and bagpipes, and the melody strings are stopped with the left hand against frets. The zither is generally placed on a table, with special feet to hold it steady. A bowed zither also appeared in Germany, but without the accompanying strings of the plucked zither.

America produced a variety of zithers, notably the Pennsylvania zither, the Appalachian dulcimer, and the Kentucky dulcimer which was bowed. The true dulcimer, as already mentioned, is not fretted and is not bowed. It had great popularity from the sixteenth to the eighteenth century in Europe, and one form, the cimbalon became the favourite instrument of gypsy orchestras, and the national instrument of Hungary. However, the early appearance of the harpsichord in the fifteenth century ensured that the psaltery and dulcimer would never hold their own against the more sophisticated and resourceful instrument.

Harps

The chief feature which distinguishes a harp from a lyre is that the plane of the strings is at an angle to the soundbox, and not parallel to it, as in the lyre. In Mesopotamia in the middle of the third millennium BC there were two main kinds of harp; the arched harp, in which the arm or neck which carries the strings is simply an upward continuation of the soundbox, and the angular harp, in which the neck is at an angle to the soundbox. The first type was also current in India, where it was played with a plectrum, and Burma, without a plectrum, but now survives only in Northern Africa and

Right: a theorbo player by Jan Bronckhorst, 1603–61.
Below: an allegorical painting of love or spring, by an anonymous Flemish artist of about 1600, in the Kunsthistorisches Museum, Vienna. Love is shown as a young lutenist sitting under a tree in a spring landscape. There are various pieces of games and sports equipment on the grass around him, with books devoted to the art of love, as well as musical partbooks. At left is a four-stringed viol with frets and a bent-back head, with its bow and a black cornett next to it. At right is a cittern, and a very sumptuous case for the lute. There are two more lutenists in the right background.

Left: a lyre player from the mosaic Standard of Ur in the British Museum, from a scene depicting a banquet. It dates from about 2600 BC, and the height of the band is approximately 5 cms. On this side of the standard are scenes of peaceful events, and on the other scenes of war.

Below: a five-stringed 8th-century *biwa* from the ancient imperial storehouse of the Nara dynasty. The biwa was the Japanese version of the short lute, which arrived in the country from China, where it was known as *p'i-p'a*.

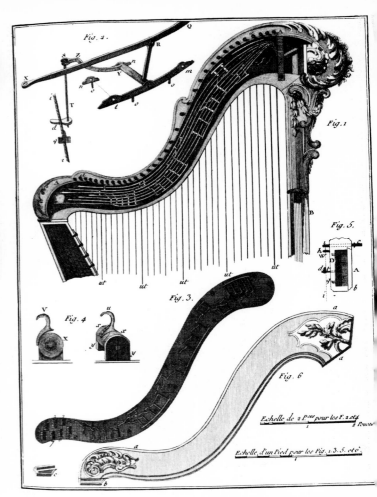

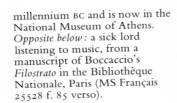

Right: an Egyptian wooden figure of a girl playing a harp, dating from the 19th Dynasty, about 1200 BC, from the British Museum.

Top centre and opposite: details of the mechanism of a single action harp with pedals, from Diderot and D'Alembert's *Encyclopédie.* The tuning key is shown as well as the hook mechanism, the pegs, and the internal arrangement of levers and springs. Originally the hooks affected only one string when activated by hand, but the pedal mechanism worked the strings of the same pitch in every octave.

Below centre: a Cycladic marble statue of a harpist from the Island of Keros. It dates from the third

millennium BC and is now in the National Museum of Athens.

Opposite below: a sick lord listening to music, from a manuscript of Boccaccio's *Filostrato* in the Bibliothèque Nationale, Paris (MS Français 25528 f. 85 verso).

Afghanistan, in a much smaller form. At the beginning of the second millennium BC in Mesopotamia an innovation was made with the introduction of the horizontal harp, which initially may simply have been an adaptation of the playing position of the arched harp. The vertical harp was plucked by the fingers of both hands, whereas the horizontal harp was plucked with a plectrum, whilst the left hand deadened or damped the strings which were not to be sounded.

The Egyptian arched harp was closely related to that of Mesopotamia, but a smaller harp with a foot was developed, as well as a small shoulder harp. The angular harp was also current in Egypt. In Greece the harp was angular and vertical, but it was always regarded as a foreign instrument, and this was true of Rome also. It was introduced into China at the end of the fourth century AD but never really established itself there. Curiously enough the harp was one of the few Asiatic instruments not introduced directly into medieval Europe. Exactly how it arrived remains a source for speculation. There is much to be said for the theory of its dissemination from Ireland, since the Irish were extraordinarily

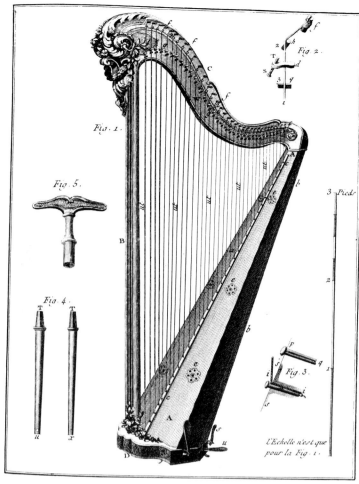

ubiquitous, even in the sixth century AD. Gozbert, in his life of St Gall, said: 'Of late so many Irish are pilgrims that it would appear that the habit of travelling is part of their nature.' The early Irish bishops were not attached to a particular diocese, as has been the tradition of the Church, but also wandered incessantly. However, even if the Irish are credited with having brought the harp to Europe, the question is not settled as to whether it was a completely independent instrument or had connections, via traders, with the Near and Middle East.

In Ireland and England the harp dates back certainly to the eleventh century AD. In accordance with general medieval practice, it was played from the left shoulder. On the Continent, however, and certainly from the time of the Renaissance, the harp was played from the right shoulder. The body of the Irish harp was always carved from a single piece of wood, willow being a very common choice, though the back of the instrument was a different piece of wood, usually pine. A great tradition of wandering minstrels existed, and the harp was their accompanying instrument. In fact the adoption of the harp as an amateur instrument was a much later development.

On the Continent of Europe the Renaissance harp was a much lighter affair. It developed later as a folk instrument, and from Spain it was taken to South America, where it has developed in a completely independent way. From a musical point of view, however, it was quite obvious that if the harp was to be incorporated into ensembles, it had to be capable of chromaticism, that is playing semitones. One of the early solutions was to add a second set of strings, and then a third one, to enable the player to introduce the necessary sharps and flats. These experiments produced double- and triple-strung harps. Another idea was to use a hook to lift the string and so raise its pitch. In element, however, this is hardly a very flexible method. But it pointed the way to the next development, and the one which was ultimately to produce the concert harp of today, and that was the introduction of pedals. Apparently the development took place in Bavaria in the second quarter of the eighteenth century. It was in France, however, that the process was fully elaborated, and by 1770 the French harps had seven pedals and the C strings were red and the F strings blue, as they are to this day, to help the player identify them quickly. Subsequent developments were simply refinements of the way in which the string was held. Eventually the hook gave way to a much more efficient system invented by Erard which was simply a disc with two projecting pins between which the string passed. When the disc was rotated by the pedal, the string was pulled by the pins, and so the tension was increased and the pitch raised.

Before leaving the harps, mention should be made of an instrument – the Aeolian harp – which is not, technically, a harp at all. It is in element a soundbox with gut or wire strings, and in this respect is more related to zithers and psalteries. Instead of being played, the 'harp' is left to vibrate in the wind, rather on the lines of the wind bells so popular in the last century.

Opposite: a painting by Mauzaisse after Giroust, now at Versailles, showing Madame de Genlis giving a harp lesson to her daughter and to Princess Adélaïde of Orleans. In addition to her abilities as a teacher of the harp, Madame de Genlis was the author of several books on general education, and was the governess of all the children of Philippe-Egalité. The harp was thought especially suitable for young ladies of breeding to demonstrate their skills upon, long after the hurdy-gurdy fell into oblivion. Although the Duke of Orleans went to the scaffold at the Revolution, his son became king as Louis-Philippe.

Above: a portrait of the guitarist Pagans, with Auguste de Gas, by Degas in the Jeu de Paume, Paris. The present popularity of the guitar throughout the Western world is simply a wheel which has turned full circle. In the Mediterranean countries of Western Europe, however, it never fell into oblivion, and in Spain in particular inspired several eminent composers to write for it, and so give it a role on the concert platform over and above its role as a folk instrument. The name of Segovia will probably be remembered as that of one of the most gifted exponents of recent times.

Wind Instruments

Most wind instruments belong either to the brass or to the woodwind group, of which a section is shown here in action with the BBC Symphony Orchestra. The brass are usually more in evidence during a symphony concert, both visually and aurally, since they are generally placed towards the back of the orchestra, in a raised position, and it is therefore easier to associate the instruments with their sounds, since the section includes trumpets, trombones and French horns. The woodwind tend to be placed at ground level, behind the strings, and it is often only when the flute or oboe has a solo passage, or the piccolo tops the orchestral texture, that we are aware of their existence. With such a subtle orchestrator as Ravel, however, the woodwind section often has a crucial role to play in the overall effect.

All wind instruments are sounded by having air blown into them, and the sound is produced by vibrations in the airstream. Basically there are three types of action involved. In the first type, an example of which is the flute, the player's lips do not generate the vibration in the airstream directly. In the second, the oboe for example, a reed vibrates in the airstream. In the third the lips vibrate and become an essential part of the sound-producing process, a good example being the trumpet. The main division of wind instruments is into wood and brass, though there are some instruments which fall between the two, as we shall see later.

Early flutes and pipes

Whistles and pipes are probably the most familiar of musical instruments and the most widespread throughout the world. Certainly the pipe is one of the oldest instruments. The Sumerians had a long, vertical pipe, and rim-blown vertical pipes were known in Egypt in the Old and Middle Kingdoms, since they are depicted on wall paintings of the time. The rim-blown pipe is still found in North Africa, the Middle East and the Balkans, but it never caught on in Europe. Double pipes, represented later in Greece by the aulos and the tibia in Rome, were also known in Mesopotamia at this time.

The double pipes of the Ancient World all seem to have been reed instruments. In other words, even if they were made of metal or wood, bamboo or bone, they were still sounded with a reed made from a slice of cane. The way a reed instrument sounds depends on the bore of the body of the instrument. If the bore is cylindrical, that is, straight up and down, then it tends to give a low, rich sound. If it is conical, however, the sound is higher pitched. Some instruments look as if they have a conical bore by their exterior form, but may well be cylindrical internally. The reed itself is either a single slice of cane, as in the modern clarinet, or double, as in the modern oboe, and the Greek and Roman double pipes seem to have had double reeds. The double reed, controlled by the lips, can give much more subtlety of tone than the single reed when not lip controlled.

There seems to have been an extremely wide variety of techniques for playing these instruments, which is rather surprising to the modern instrumentalist who is so used to playing his instrument in an accepted way. From the surviving evidence it is by no means clear how the various pipes were

Below: a Benin bronze figurine in the British Museum of a dignitary or a priest blowing a pipe very much akin to a transverse flute.
Top: the Troparium of St Martial in the Bibliothèque Nationale, Paris, shows 12th-century musicians beside Gregorian melodies. Here a juggler is accompanied by a double reed pipe.
Bottom: a young man playing a set of double pipes from a painted Etruscan frieze in the Tomb of the Leopards at Tarquinia.
Opposite: a detail showing a man playing bagpipes from *Peasant Dance* by Pieter Breughel the Elder *c.* 1520–69, now in the Kunsthistorisches Museum, Vienna.

intended to be played, however, though from the arrangement of the holes for the fingers, one can assume that in some versions one pipe played the tune whilst the other provided a kind of drone. At the other end of the scale, both pipes had exactly the same number of holes, in the same positions, with the pipes parallel to each other, so that both sets of holes could be stopped or covered with the fingers of one hand. In between are several combinations providing ample opportunity for rhythmic and harmonic variety.

Flutes were also common in the Far East and still are in many places. One of the frequent depictions of the Indian god Krishna is as a flautist, and several varieties of flute were known in China and Japan. The wall paintings in the Tunghuang caves, which date from the T'ang dynasty (618–907 AD), show an instrumental ensemble which includes a set of pan pipes, a pipe played vertically, which may be a kind of oboe, and transverse flutes, that is flutes which are played horizontally. There is a rather beautiful poem by the ninth-century government official Po Chü-i in which the author laments the fact that the lute is being abandoned in favour of the flute and zithern, which were not classical instruments in China at that time. Po Chü-i seems to have been rather apt to latch onto images which expressed his melancholy, and take them as signs of the general decay of things. The lute however was not originally an instrument native to China, as we saw in the previous chapter, and despite the fact that it became the national instrument of China in the shape of the p'i-p'a, and was a classical instrument by the time Po Chü-i was alive, it really had no stronger claim than the flute and zithern were soon to have.

Hornpipes and bagpipes

A quite distinct form of an early reed instrument is the hornpipe, which has nothing to do with the dance of the same name. If one thinks of the hornpipe dance tunes that one knows, they are typically violin-type tunes, and scarcely ideal for reed instruments. The hornpipe as instrument, then, is a reed pipe with a horn, usually that of a cow, on the end of it – hence the name. Sometimes, particularly in Eastern Europe, they were fitted up with a skin or airtight bag or bellows to make bagpipes. The principle of the instrument is basically the same, however; it is merely the nature of the wind supply which has altered.

There is evidence that bagpipes were known in the Near East about the same time as Christianity began to take root, but oddly enough they then seem to have gone into a decline and did not reappear until the Middle Ages. It is possible that they were lost entirely for a time and were more or less rediscovered during that period. In Eastern Europe the bagpipe sound tends to be smoother and clearer than the Western European variety, of which the Scottish pipes are probably the best known. The Eastern pipes have cylindrical bores, and those of the West conical bores, giving a much more shrill sound, with lots of overtones. The English Northumbrian pipes, however, are softer and give an altogether more refined sound.

A Tiahuanaco pipe (*opposite*) in the shape of a man playing a pipe and (*above*) a Bolivian panpipe carved from stone, now in the Natural History Museum, New York. The early pipes, though undoubtedly the forerunners of our modern wind instruments, were nevertheless soon left behind as man developed his society and discovered new musical techniques. Consequently such instruments soon became associated with rustic and pastoral peoples, and were rather forgotten by the mainstream of musical development.

The Scottish pipes consist of a pipe through which the air is blown into a leather bag, and four reed pipes. Of these four pipes, three are drones, of fixed pitch. The fourth pipe, known as the chaunter, plays the tune; the player controlling the notes by means of fingerholes in the body of the chaunter which is a double reed. The pressure of air is kept up by the player's elbow against the bag, which is held under the arm. The Irish pipes have two drones only–corresponding to the two highest drones of the Scottish pipes. This means that they have a more shrill sound than the Scottish pipes.

Although in the Middle Ages they were used extensively, almost anywhere, bagpipes now have a close association with shepherds and the countryside, and both Bach and Handel, amongst others, evoke them for the shepherds in the Christmas music in *The Christmas Oratorio* and *Messiah* respectively. It is particularly difficult to combine bagpipes with other instruments because some of their notes are much sharper–i.e. higher pitched–than those played by orchestral instruments. They would sound disturbingly out of tune as a result. Neither composer therefore introduced them into the orchestra. Bach used a quartet of oboes against flutes, strings and continuo, and Handel three violins, viola and bass continuo strengthened with two bassoons. Both employ 12/8 time, but Bach, whose instrumentation is technically much closer to the bagpipe, writes something quite removed from shepherds. With its descending bass line, and virtually every beat of the bar broken up into dotted rhythm, it achieves something of a stately dance, which then expands into a poignant study. Handel's piece is emotionally at a much lower pitch. The whole feeling is much calmer, and the effect is one of rustic simplicity. The sustained pedal notes recall the drone of the bagpipes, appropriately aided by the bassoons, but the upper part writing is entirely for strings.

Recorders

Another very common sight in the Middle Ages and even later was the musician with pipe and tabor. The tabor is a small snare drum which the player beats with his right hand, and with his left he plays the pipe. This pipe, with only two holes on top for the fingers and one underneath for the thumb, was the forerunner of the recorder. In between came the flageolet, which had six main fingerholes, two of which were underneath.

The recorder brought more subtle tonal quality and fingering technique, as a result of which the pipe began to take leave of the realm of folk music and go indoors, as it were, to more refined music making. Whole consorts of recorders

Right: an ivory carving by Christof Angermaier, court artist at Munich early in the 17th century. In the left foreground is a bass recorder, with cornett and racket behind; in the centre background a pommer, crumhorn and flute, and in the right foreground a trombone, bagpipes, descant pommer and panpipes.
Above: an elephant carrying musicians in a procession to welcome Richard of Cornwall to Cremona in 1241, recorded by Matthew Paris. Two trumpets, a drum and a pair of double pipes can be seen, and the man in charge of the elephant rings a large handbell.
Opposite: a panel from a carved wooden lectern in the Bieck Museum, Poland, about 1633, showing town musicians playing cornett, bass recorder and trumpet.

were introduced, and the instruments had a position among woodwind very similar to that of the viols amongst stringed instruments. There are seven fingerholes on top and one underneath, and on the large bass instruments the last fingerhole usually has a key to cover it. The early or Renaissance recorders were of one piece, whereas the later Baroque recorders were in three pieces, and this has been followed down to the present time, except for the tiny descant recorder, which is of one piece. Because of its use as a music teaching instrument, the descant recorder today has a prominence it never had previously, since it was for the next size down, so to speak – the treble recorder – that Bach and Handel wrote their flute parts. It was then known as a flauto dolce. The flute to which we are now accustomed was known as a flauto traverso or German flute. To avoid any confusion here we will continue to use the term flute exclusively for the transverse flute.

Consorts of flutes were also used at the Renaissance, and flutes were apparently used as solo instruments with strings to form consorts. Like recorders, Renaissance flutes were of one piece, and later Baroque models were of three, and then four, joints or sections. Flutes were made of ebony, boxwood, or even glass, though silver is now the preferred material. However, before moving on to the modern orchestral versions

of these instruments, there are one or two which are obsolete or have been revived, and which need to be looked at.

Curtals and crumhorns

There was an old soft-toned reed instrument called curtal in English, *dolzaina* or *dulzaina* in Italian, and *douçaine* in French. It flourished in the fourteenth and fifteenth centuries apparently, and as late as 1529 was included in the band of wind instruments which played for a wedding breakfast at the ducal court in Ferrara. Its importance for us today lies in the fact that in its latest stage of development it was the forerunner of the modern bassoon.

By 1500 another reed instrument, the crumhorn, had taken the stage. Visually the crumhorn is easily recognized because its end bells out slightly and is upturned. It has been revived recently and has a quite distinctive timbre. For a singer brought up in the classical tradition and who is required to sing with crumhorns, the soft, faint buzzing tone, of slightly indeterminate focus, can be devastating to one's sense of pitch after a while. The crumhorn has a double reed and a cylindrical bore despite the slightly flared look. The player does not blow directly on the reed, however, but into a kind of cap, with an opening at the top to which the lips are applied and the reed is inside this cap.

Rackets

Another consort reed instrument was the racket, in which the bore was cut up into short sections and put side by side, rather like a bundle of sausages. This meant that a bore which would theoretically require an instrument a number of feet long could be contained in a squat cylinder less than a foot high. The irregular disposition of the fingerholes around the body looks rather as if some insect had been at work on it.

Shawms

Shawms, cornetts and serpents are the last group of instruments to be considered which are now obsolete, though the serpent lingered on into the last century, when it could occasionally be found in the galleries at the back of churches, supplementing the choir. The cornett and serpent will be considered just before the brass instruments, however, because although they were generally wooden and had fingerholes, they had cupped mouthpieces and are therefore technically more closely related to brass wind instruments.

The shawm, however, was the forerunner of the oboe. It was also known as a loud instrument, and it was held rather like a trumpet, so that the sound received maximum diffusion. By the same analogy, some organ pipes are now placed in this position – known as *en chamade* – particularly the trumpet and tuba organ stops. This position, whether blown by the player or an organ bellows, is not chiefly responsible for the loudness. It comes rather from the nature of – in the case of the shawm – the reed and the way the player uses his lips. The reed itself broadens out towards the top, that is the part nearest the player's mouth, and it is fitted into a metal tube or staple (as is the crumhorn), which is then fitted into the body of the instrument. In the East there is a disc or broad rim round the outside of the staple, and by pressing the lips closely to the rim and allowing the reed to vibrate inside the mouth, the characteristic, somewhat raucous sound is produced. In the West the disc was replaced by a series of rings known as a pirouette. This has the effect of giving the player more scope to use his lips, and yet it still leaves the reed free to vibrate.

Bass shawms were known as pommers on the Continent, and they enjoyed considerable success during the sixteenth century, but fell into obscurity during the seventeenth.

64

MODERN WOODWIND INSTRUMENTS

In the modern symphony orchestra the woodwind instruments are usually the least visible to the audience in the normal concert hall. The players generally sit behind the strings in the centre of the orchestra, and are not as high up as the brass and percussion sections, so that one tends to be aware of them

A modern flute and piccolo. The flute's natural scale is D, and it can sound roughly three successive octaves up from middle C on the piano. The piccolo is the highest woodwind instrument of the orchestra and is a small flute which sounds an octave above the normal flute. Its music is written an octave lower than it sounds.

Top: The transverse flute from Bonanni's *Gabinetto armonico* (1723) was still basically that developed by the French in the

chiefly when they have solo passages. Even then, it is very difficult to see where exactly the sound is coming from, let alone which particular instrument is playing at that moment.

Flutes

The flutes are recognizable because they are held across the player's face, and he blows across the instrument, rather than placing it in his mouth. The early flutes were of cylindrical bore, but during the seventeenth century, as the instrument evolved, the tendency was for the head section (or joint, as it is known) only to remain cylindrical, and the other three became conical. Because the flautist blows across the hole in his instrument, and does not apply his lips directly to it as with, for example, the whistle mouthpiece of the recorder, he has much more scope for nuance and interpretation. That is why, with the onset of the Romantic tendencies in music, it filled a role in which the recorder could never hope to emulate it. There are considerable technical difficulties involved in playing the flute in certain keys, and the one in which the instrument is most at home is D Major. Basically the problem arises from the fact that whereas with stringed instruments it is possible to play the consecutive notes of a scale moving up and down the strings, and producing harmonics as a kind of optional extra, with wind instruments the harmonics are needed as an integral part of the scale. In fact Joachim Quantz, who taught Frederick the Great how to play the flute, maintained that the flautist should only play solos in the difficult keys if the audience knew exactly what was involved. However, if the flute was to become a fully fledged member of the orchestra, it had to have complete adaptability to whatever key it might be called upon to play. The music of Beethoven, with its tendencies towards a complete disintegration of classical tonality, hastened this development. The solution was obviously more keys on the instrument, and more efficient keys at that.

As far as the flute was concerned, the right man appeared in the right place at the right time – or rather two men. One was the English flautist Charles Nicholson (1795–1837), whose beautiful tone inspired the other, the Bavarian Theobald Boehm (1794–1881) to carry out a complete rationalization of the instrument. Boehm had been trained as a jeweller, but

was principal flautist in the orchestra at Munich and a soloist of note in his own right. On a visit to London he heard Nicholson play, and by 1832 he had produced his new model. This flute had a conical bore, as had most flutes of his day, but he had altered the position of the fingerholes and introduced ring keys, by which a player can cover a hole and at the same time operate a key with it. Some fifteen years later he reverted to a cylindrical bore with a parabolic head. (A parabola is produced when a slice is made through a cone parallel to its side.) It is this model which, apart from minute modifications, is now the modern flute. It was rapidly taken up in France and England, though in Germany it was slow to catch on. Wagner for one did not like it, but then his opinion of Bavarians and things Bavarian was never very high, despite the fact that they saved him from disaster through the generosity of their king, Ludwig II.

Before leaving the flute, mention must be made of the piccolo, which is in reality a small flute, sounding an octave higher than the normal flute. It also has Boehm's mechanism, but with a conical bore, that is, like Boehm's first flute model. There is a tendency now, however, to follow suit and produce piccolos with cylindrical bores. Bass flutes (often confusingly called alto flutes), also exist in a modern form, though they are rarely called for in the orchestral repertoire. They have been used to interesting effect in some jazz combinations. The fife is now the name usually given to the Bb flute. It has a cylindrical bore and no keys, and is often used with drums to make up the fife and drum band.

Oboes and bassoons

The shawm, as we have already seen, was a forerunner of the oboe, but the instrument as we know it now can be said to have been invented in 1660 or thereabouts by Jean Hotteterre and Michel Philidor in France, and it was Lully, a French composer of Italian origin, who first wrote for it. When Purcell wrote his *Ode for the Birthday of Queen Mary* ('Come Ye Sons of Art'), in 1694, he used the oboe extensively, and to excellent effect, considering how new an instrument it was. But it was its refinement which made the instrument such a success so quickly. The refinement came partly from the longer, narrower double reed, and partly from the boring, which was more accurate because the oboe was in three parts, whereas the old shawms had been in one piece. The bore was narrower, too, which meant that the rather raucous effect of the shawm, imparted by the overtone, was cut down and a much purer sound produced. One can see in Purcell's ode, for example, that the clear, incisive quality appealed to him very much, and he uses it for the sprightly introductory theme which has a somewhat martial flavour and also for the soprano solo, 'Bid the Graces', which is virtually a duet between instrument and voice, sometimes answering each other, sometimes weaving in and out in close suspensions, and sometimes together in seemingly endless coloratura phrases.

At the same time as the modern oboe emerged there was also a tenor oboe, which may be the oboe da caccia (literally hunting oboe) for which Bach wrote. On the other hand, the

previous century. It had one key on the foot joint, and a slightly conical bore running in the opposite direction from that shown here. In other words, it was wider at the mouthpiece end,

and narrower at the foot. The older flute, which is what Bonanni actually described, had a cylindrical bore, and Theobald Boehm reintroduced the cylindrical bore in the 19th century.

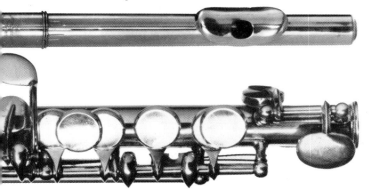

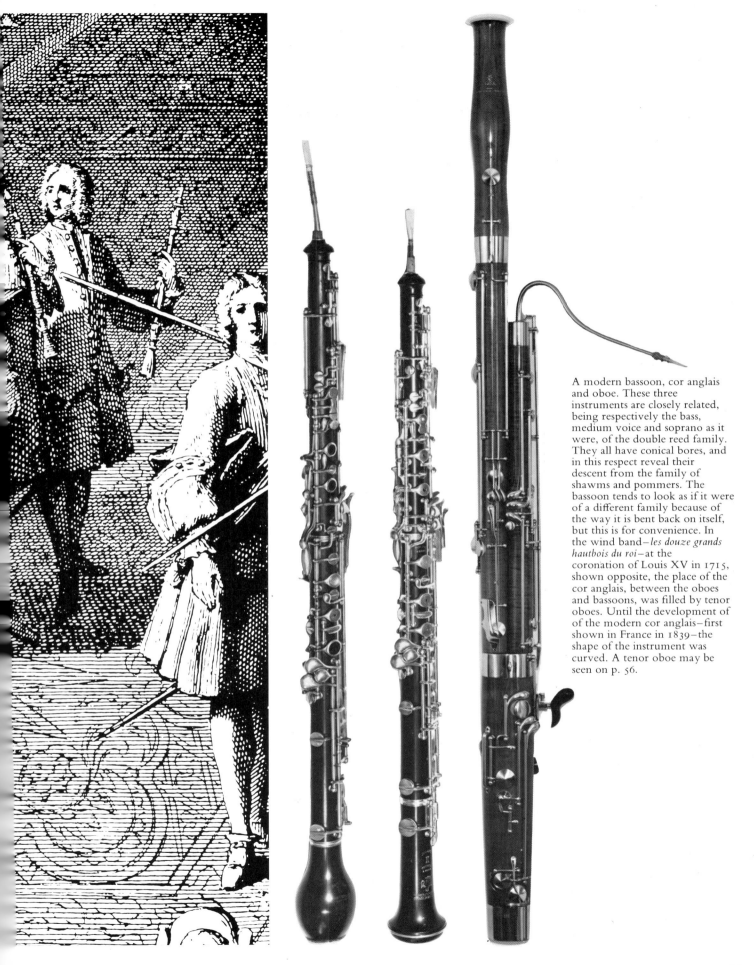

A modern bassoon, cor anglais and oboe. These three instruments are closely related, being respectively the bass, medium voice and soprano as it were, of the double reed family. They all have conical bores, and in this respect reveal their descent from the family of shawms and pommers. The bassoon tends to look as if it were of a different family because of the way it is bent back on itself, but this is for convenience. In the wind band – *les douze grands hautbois du roi* – at the coronation of Louis XV in 1715, shown opposite, the place of the cor anglais, between the oboes and bassoons, was filled by tenor oboes. Until the development of of the modern cor anglais – first shown in France in 1839 – the shape of the instrument was curved. A tenor oboe may be seen on p. 56.

The bell of a fine early Dutch
oboe which dates from the late
17th century. A consort of
musicians in contemporary
costume are playing two oboes,
tenor oboe and bassoon and
reading from part books on the
table. It has also been suggested
that this oboe might be French.

instrument may have been the cor anglais (literally English horn), which may be regarded as a tenor oboe, though with a distinctive timbre. Between the oboe and the cor anglais is the oboe d'amore, a third below the normal oboe. It disappeared towards the end of the eighteenth century and was revived specifically for Bach performances in the last two decades of the last century and the early part of the present century. The symphony referred to earlier in *The Christmas Oratorio* calls for two oboes of each sort–da caccia and d'amore. Another member of the family is the hecklephone or baritone oboe, invented by Wilhelm Heckel.

The bassoon, which developed from the curtal, is really a kind of bass oboe. The sound it produces, however, would not immediately make one think of it as a close relative of the oboe. Of the *douze grands hautbois du roi* (the king in this case being Louis XIV), two were in fact bassoons. The conical bore of the bassoon is in four joints and has an extension at the bottom bent back on itself to save space. Otherwise it would require an unmanageably long instrument. There is no doubt also that the extra thickness of wood gives added tonal resonance to the instrument. The double reed does not go directly into the body, but there is a curved brass mouthpiece known as a crook. The French model enjoyed great popularity until Wilhelm Heckel (1856–1909), of heckelphone fame, in Germany carried out a rationalization of the instrument which is now most commonly used throughout the world, except in Southwestern Europe from Belgium down through France and Spain to Italy. The contrabassoon or double bassoon is pitched an octave below the bassoon, and treble and tenor bassoons also exist. The player may suspend the instrument from a strap around his neck, or else have a metal tail-pin, similar to that of the 'cello. There is much to be said for a new attempt being made at a further and more radical rationalization of the bassoon.

Clarinets

The clarinet was invented by Johann Christoff Denner (1655–1707) in Nuremberg in the early years of the eighteenth century. In the world of musical instruments it is extremely rare to be able to be so categoric as to time, place and date, but the clarinet is an exception. The instrument has a cylindrical bore, and a single reed which is bound or clipped onto the mouthpiece. In the early method of playing, the reed was on the upper side of the mouthpiece, and the top lip controlled the vibration. The classic French method (known as embouchure) involves using the lips as cushions between the teeth and the mouthpiece, with the reed on the under side of it. The Boehm system for the flute was applied to the clarinet, and this is the one used today.

The basset horn is a kind of tenor clarinet, though with the same sort of reservations made on p. 57 about the cor anglais being a tenor oboe–it is not quite accurate as a description. Early basset horns were bent at an angle in the middle so as to shorten the overall length of the instrument, and therefore the distance the player would have to stretch to reach the lower keys. This, and the bell at the end where the

Below: Papalini's bass clarinet in the museum of the Paris Conservatoire. This instrument is something of a curiosity, as its very appearance would suggest, but constitutes a serious attempt to compress some of the length needed for a normal bass clarinet (*left*). Although called the bass clarinet, this is not in fact the largest member of the family. There are much larger clarinets in existence–in particular the giant octo-contrabass.

Centre: saxophones are single reed wind instruments made of brass. They were designed round about 1840 and soon introduced into French army bands; indeed they were particularly useful in this context, because they bridged the gap between the orchestral wind and brass. There is a whole family of saxophones, from soprano to bass. Seen here are baritone, alto and soprano.

sound is emitted, gives the early instrument a curiously unstable or experimental appearance, and yet Mozart was particularly fond of the timbre and used two basset horns in his *Requiem*.

Alto (also known as tenor), bass and contrabass clarinets have been made and used from time to time, though without winning any large following.

We now come to a group of instruments which are reed instruments and yet are made of brass.

Saxophones

The most common of these brass-reeds to the majority of readers will probably be the saxophone, which is a single reed instrument with keys, but made of brass. It was designed by Adolphe Sax, of Belgian origin, round about 1840, and was soon taken up by French military bands. The mouthpiece is rather similar to that of the clarinet, but the bore is conical. There are soprano, alto, tenor, baritone and bass saxophones, but the middle three are the most popular. They have rarely been scored for in classical music, though the passage in Ravel's *Bolero* should be familiar to most people, particularly those who are ballet lovers.

A double reed brass instrument, much on the lines of the saxophone, was invented by Sarrus, a Frenchman, and called the sarrusophone. It never caught on, however, possibly through the influence of Sax, who was well-connected in the military music field.

As there are brass-reed instruments, there are also wood-wind instruments played, not with a reed, but with the cupped mouthpiece characteristic of brass instruments.

Cornett and Serpent

The cornett, spelled in this way to avoid confusion with the modern brass instrument known as a cornet, reached the peak of its popularity in the seventeenth century, and then declined. The body of the instrument was eight-sided, and usually made out of two lengthwise pieces which were covered with leather. However, there was also a straight cornett, known as a mute cornett because of its covered tone, which had its mouthpiece as an integral part of the instrument. Although it was usually made of wood, or sometimes ivory, it seems to have evolved

The modern flute was largely the result of the efforts of the Bavarian Theobald Boehm – himself an accomplished flautist – who carried out various experiments in the early part of the 19th century that produced the versatile keyed instrument that we know today. Seen here is the internationally famous flautist James Galway.

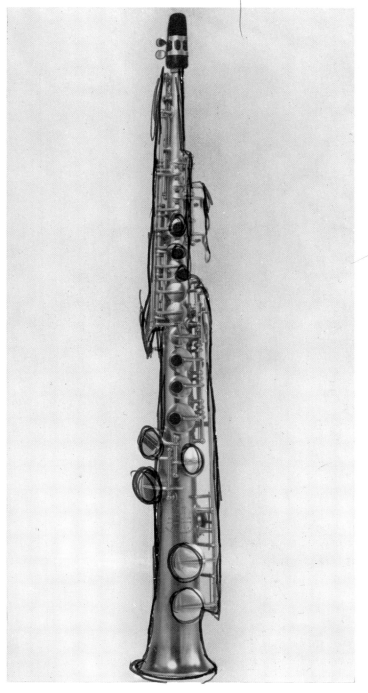

from a simple cow horn. The curved shape of the cornett would seem to bear this out, and the mouthpieces were frequently made of horn, or again ivory.

It is the mouthpiece which distinguishes the cornett from reed instruments. The principle is that of all brass mouthpieces, namely that the breath of the player is propelled through the lips into a cupped mouthpiece. Instead of a reed, however, it is the player's own lips which vibrate. There are fingerholes on the body of the instrument, and despite its apparently primitive aspect, those who were able to play it – and Benvenuto Cellini was one of the more surprising performers on the cornett – could produce remarkably subtle effects.

The serpent was more or less the larger version of the cornett, and had keys added to it during the latter part of the eighteenth century and a brass crook similar to that of the bassoon, between the mouthpiece and the body of the instrument. The shape which is so characteristic is a fascinating field for speculation, but its primary function was yet another answer to the age-old problem as to how to get maximum length of bore in the least space. The racket was one solution, the bassoon another. More suitable ones for brass instruments, as we shall now see, are coiling and the use of the slide.

49

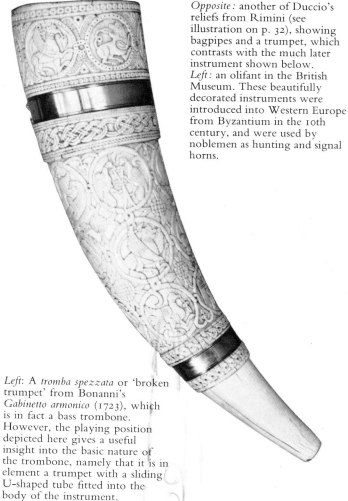

Opposite: another of Duccio's reliefs from Rimini (see illustration on p. 32), showing bagpipes and a trumpet, which contrasts with the much later instrument shown below.
Left: an olifant in the British Museum. These beautifully decorated instruments were introduced into Western Europe from Byzantium in the 10th century, and were used by noblemen as hunting and signal horns.

Left: A *tromba spezzata* or 'broken trumpet' from Bonanni's *Gabinetto armonico* (1723), which is in fact a bass trombone. However, the playing position depicted here gives a useful insight into the basic nature of the trombone, namely that it is in element a trumpet with a sliding U-shaped tube fitted into the body of the instrument.

BRASS INSTRUMENTS

Coming to the brass instruments proper, one notices one very basic element, and that is the signal call, whether it be the brassy, martial sound of the trumpet or the softer call of the horn. Simplifying matters as far as possible, one can say that the animal horn inspired the softer brass instruments, of which the modern French horn is probably the most familiar example. These instruments have a funnel-shaped mouthpiece and a conical bore. In antiquity the Jewish shofar, made from a ram's horn, and the Roman buccina, tuba and cornu were probably all in this tradition. Trumpet-like instruments, however, have a much more truly brassy sound. The bore is cylindrical and the mouthpiece hemispherical. The bell shape at the end of the instrument amplifies and at the same time refines the timbre. The long, thin Roman lituus, with its crooked end, is a forerunner of this tradition. The modern tuba comes more or less between the horns and trumpets, having the conical bore of the horn and a more horn-like tone, but the hemispherical mouthpiece of the trumpet.

We are used now to thinking of brass as instruments capable of playing whole melodies, but this is a comparatively recent development. That is why so much early classical music for trumpets is in the key of D, because it is basically the natural key for the instrument. One might almost say that the whole history of the development of brass instruments has been a series of attempts to exploit the exciting quality of the sound so that it could be used much more widely, and not just as bugle calls in certain pieces of music in a particular key. That is why the cornett was such an important bridge. It showed that a cupped mouthpiece, with fingerholes in the body of the instrument, was one way of achieving the desired flexibility. Effectively, when one closes or stops a fingerhole, one is shortening the length of the sounding tube, which is of fixed length. The other development retained the mouthpiece and sounding tube of fixed length, but instead of shortening it, the idea was to lengthen it, and so the trombone was born, with its characteristic slide. Obviously the slide effect could only be introduced into an instrument with a bore of uniform diameter – a cylindrical bore – and therefore with the trumpet type of instrument. These early trombones were known as sackbuts in medieval England, and posaunen in

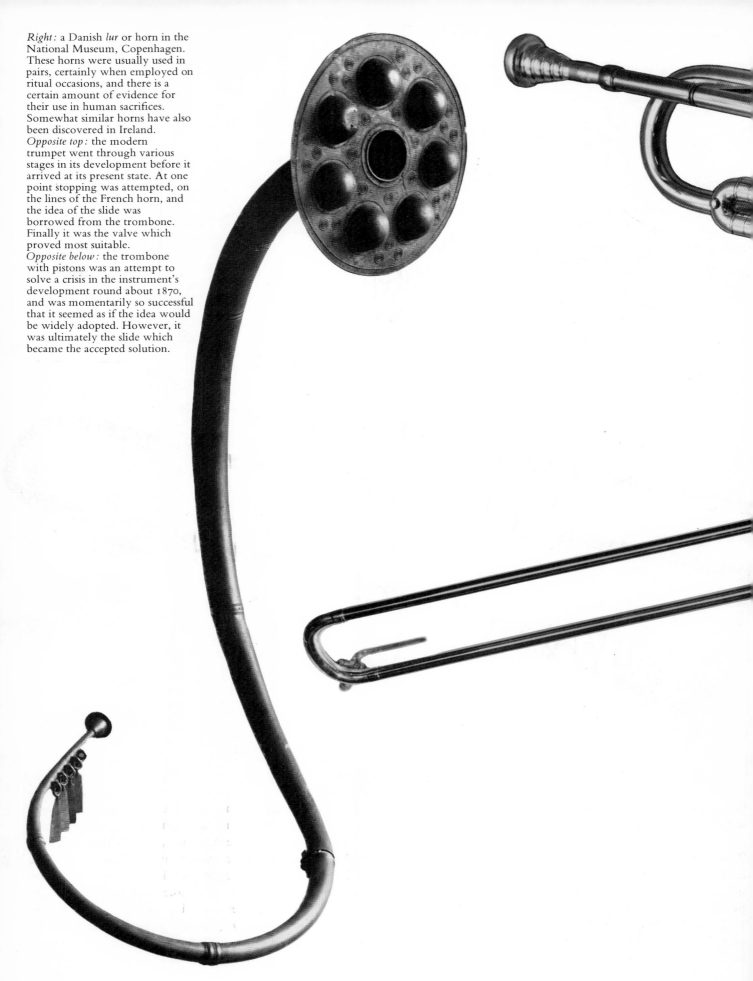

Right: a Danish *lur* or horn in the National Museum, Copenhagen. These horns were usually used in pairs, certainly when employed on ritual occasions, and there is a certain amount of evidence for their use in human sacrifices. Somewhat similar horns have also been discovered in Ireland.

Opposite top: the modern trumpet went through various stages in its development before it arrived at its present state. At one point stopping was attempted, on the lines of the French horn, and the idea of the slide was borrowed from the trombone. Finally it was the valve which proved most suitable.

Opposite below: the trombone with pistons was an attempt to solve a crisis in the instrument's development round about 1870, and was momentarily so successful that it seemed as if the idea would be widely adopted. However, it was ultimately the slide which became the accepted solution.

Germany, and the instrument has altered little since then. It is rather the playing technique which has evolved.

Trumpets

Slides were also introduced for trumpets, though not with a great deal of success, and whereas the trombone solved its problem early on, the trumpet had to wait until about 1815, with the introduction of valves, before it became as versatile an instrument as we now know it. There was a keyed trumpet in the eighteenth century – Haydn's Trumpet Concerto was written for it – but it was the valve which was to be the answer to the problem. The principle behind the valve is basically the same as the slide of the trombone, namely that the length of the sounding tube is increased. However, instead of a long slide, the extra tube is cut up into sections or loops, so that the depressing of each valve adds more sounding tube to the instrument, and so lowers the pitch. There was no logical reason why valves which raised the pitch should not be introduced also, but they are either used very little nowadays or not at all.

A French horn made in Paris round about 1825 by M. A. Raoux. It is of brass with silver mounts and the inside of the bell is painted with green and gilt lacquer.

Opposite: a six-pistoned bass tuba Saxhorn. Developed by Adolphe Sax of saxophone fame, the family of saxhorns have had little effect on the orchestral instruments, except for the tuba.

Horns

We mentioned previously some of the early horns, but it is doubtful whether they had any direct influence on the immediate predecessors of modern horns, namely the hunting horns dating from the sixteenth century, whose distinctive feature was the fact that they were coiled. In the mid-seventeenth century several attempts were made in France to improve the instruments, and instead of several coils, two were used and, towards the end of the century, one only. Horns suffered from the same problem as early trumpets, namely that they could only be used in one key. One answer was to have several horns, and another was to have coiled crooks of different lengths which fitted between the mouthpiece and the instrument proper. This still had its disadvantages, however, since it was obviously a very cumbersome system, and it would not have survived into the days of frequent modulation or changes of tonality within a single piece of music.

Then in the middle of the eighteenth century a horn player from Dresden, Anton Josef Hampel, discovered during experimentation with mutes that if he pushed a mute, in this case a wad of cotton, into the bell, the pitch of the instrument dropped, then when the wad was in as far as it would go, the pitch rose a semitone. He found that he achieved exactly the same effect with his hand without the cotton, and that the tone of the instrument was much smoother. This, then, is how the horn technique evolved. Following on from there, Hampel saw that the question of changing crooks was impossible if both hands were to be occupied – one to hold the instrument and the other to mute it – so he redesigned the instrument with a fixed mouthpiece and crooks in the centre of the coil. This had the disadvantage that the muted notes sounded wildly different from the open or unmuted notes. The valve was once more the saviour of the situation, however, and it was quickly brought into use for the horn. One of the most frequently adopted solutions nowadays is that of the double horn – in other words an instrument with a set of coils (or slides) for a horn in F and a set of coils for a horn in B♭, operated by three valves, with a fourth valve, operated by the thumb, to switch from one to the other.

Horn players, particularly third and fourth horns, get long periods of rest in the course of certain pieces of music. They probably rank second only to percussion players for the amount of bars rest they have. On the other hand, the horns also have some of the most cruelly exposed solo passages in the repertoire, for example the notorious cadenza in Beethoven's Ninth Symphony, and usually earn their rest.

Bugle and Cornet

The bugle was another instrument to be fitted with valves, though for a while it was fitted with keys, and a keyed bass bugle, called an ophicleide, was also produced. However, its place was taken by another valved instrument, the cornet, which began life as the European post horn. Despite the fact that great cornet players have emerged from time to time, it has always been rather looked down upon as an instrument. It has never quite shaken off its more popular associations and has consequently never become established as a member of the orchestra. Certainly it is an easier instrument to play than the trumpet, which is its closest rival, but in all fairness to the trumpet and the trumpet player, one must admit that it does not have the tonal distinction and dignity of the trumpet.

In the wake of the bugle, a number of valved instruments have followed, notably the tuba or, when a tenor tuba, the euphonium. The ubiquitous Adolphe Sax designed a whole family of valved horns known as saxhorns, and a saxtromba. In reality Sax did little but standardize the existing instruments, but what was gained in efficiency and co-ordination was generally felt to have been lost in quality of timbre.

Percussion Instruments

Of all the percussion instruments, the timpani look the most spectacular, since they are usually placed centrally, at the back of the orchestra, dominating it visually, and capable of making important rhythmic and textural contributions, as well as playing some spectacular solo passages, as in Beethoven's Ninth Symphony, for example. Seen here is the BBC Symphony Orchestra's David Stirling. However, the timpani are only part of the very diverse family of percussion instruments whose sole unifying characteristic is the fact that they are struck in order to produce their sounds. Not only drums, but cymbals, gongs, tubular bells, xylophones, wood blocks, triangle, castanets and tambourines go to make up this most colourful section of the orchestra.

Nowadays the term percussion stands for a very distinctive group of instruments whose place in the modern orchestra is to provide colour and texture to the instrumentation, or to accentuate the rhythms. A percussion player has to be something of a musical jack of all trades. In a symphony orchestra you may see two or possibly three people in charge of an amazing array of equipment, and they usually have to be fairly agile to get from one instrument to another. They tend to have fevered bursts of activity and then long periods of inactivity. It is essential, therefore to be able to count bars if you think of taking up percussion. Often the instruments they use are in element among the oldest in the world. Some of them produce no recognizable note at all. Others are melodic. The only feature common to all is the act of striking or hitting–hence the term percussion.

The business of placing percussion instruments into categories is thus rather difficult. Melodic percussion instruments are those such as the xylophone, vibraphone, tubular bells, marimba, and the modern kettledrum. The word melodic is used here in the narrow sense of producing a recognizable note. It would be difficult to play a tune on a single drum. Non-melodic percussion instruments are those such as the gong, triangle, cymbals and castanets, and also drums such as the side and bass drums. It is consequently more convenient to take the drum family first, then the melodic instruments of percussion, and finally the non-melodic.

Drums

A drum is essentially an instrument in which a membrane is stretched over a frame or hollow body and struck with the hands or sticks. Early drums were simply hollowed out of tree trunks; later pottery shapes were covered with skins. Drums have always played–and to a large extent still do play –an important part in man's ritual and this testifies to the degree of closeness with which musical instruments are bound up with man's life.

Tambours or tambourines had been known from the early second millennium BC in Mesopotamia, where they may well have been connected with the cult of the Mother Goddess; the tambour was virtually always associated with women, even in later Greek and Roman times. It consists of a skin stretched over a wooden ring, and is played with the fingers striking the skin. Subsequently, jingles of bells or metal discs were attached to it. It probably came to Europe late in the

Right: a detail from one of the pilasters of the entrance to the Church of Saints Andrea and Bernardino in Perugia, by Duccio. One of the angels has a small pair of kettledrums, and the other a triangle.

Opposite: an angel musician with a tambourine, from a fresco by Benozzo Gozzoli (*c.*1421–97), who was commissioned in 1459 by Piero de' Medici to carry out the decoration of the chapel in the Medici Palace in Florence.

twelfth or early in the thirteenth century. Today it is associated almost entirely with gypsy music and the folk element, such as the Italian tarantella dance now given a new lease of life as a tourist attraction. It has its place in the orchestra, however, and has seen a brief spell of popularity lately in the trappings of the pop group.

Another drum known in Mesopotamia was the friction drum, a pot or bowl with a skin stretched over the top, and a stick passing through the skin vertically. When the stick is rubbed the deep sound emitted is rather like a series of grunts. The origin of the friction drum is taken to have been in Neolithic fertility rites. A rectangular frame drum also seems to have been in existence in Mesopotamia, and frame drums have also been found in Egypt.

It may have been from Mesopotamia that the earliest drums were taken into India, but without reliable sources one cannot say with any certainty. Later evidence – carved temple reliefs of the second century BC – would seem to indicate a subsequent Persian influence. The most common form of drum depicted is a barrel shape with skins at both ends without a hoop, but with thongs laced crosswise from the skins to a central band. Both hands and sticks were used to beat them.

The barrel drum was also common in ancient China and Japan, but in addition there was a drum filled with grain, a custom also found among North American Indians, and one with a stick passing diagonally through it with beads attached to one end. When the drum was shaken on the stick the beads beat against the skin. Later Chinese and Japanese drums fell into two main types, depending on whether the skins were secured with nails or with thongs. One of the more interesting developments in the Far East, in Burma, is the drum chime. Several tuned drums – up to twenty-four – are arranged in a circle and the player sits in the centre. With so many drums it is possible to play a tune.

Kettledrums are open hemispherical or egg-shaped instruments with a skin stretched across the top. The earliest kettledrums were probably of clay, then metal. India developed kettledrums in both silver and copper, and much smaller pottery ones. India also uses kettledrums in chamber music, which is rather unusual, though of course one should not think of the huge orchestral kettledrums of the Western symphony orchestra in this context.

It was via Persia and the Arabic world that the kettledrum came to the West, and this happened at the time of the Crusades. In fact the old word in English, nakers, is a direct attempt to render the Arabic *naqqara*, which in French became *nacaires*, and in Italian *naccheroni*. Previously, apart from the small, frame drums – the tambourine and the tabor, played together with the pipe – there was little evidence of widespread use of drums in Western Europe.

The principle point of evolution which turned the kettledrum from a rather inflexible military instrument into a firmly established member of the modern symphony orchestra was the facility with which it could be tuned. In their military context kettledrums were usually tuned to C and G or D and A to harmonize with the trumpets' C and D. Stands were

Below: a drum from Provence in southern France, which is very similar to the idea of the tabor. It has a double snare of gut over the head, and the player hangs it from his left arm and strikes it with a drumstick held in his right hand, thus leaving his left hand free to play a pipe.

designed so that the drums could be used in churches, or theatres, and during the eighteenth century kettledrums were made solely for orchestral use for the first time. They were known as timpani, which is the modern orchestral term still, though now there are three instead of the original two. The question of rapid tuning to meet the demands of the symphony orchestra was given added urgency in the light of demands from Beethoven's music, for example, and early in the nineteenth century Gerhard Cramer, in Munich, devised a system whereby a central screw acted on all the individual tuning screws at once.

Subsequently the central screw became pedal operated, so that it is now possible for a timpanist to raise the pitch of his drums a whole octave in a matter of seconds. Next time you see a symphony orchestra in action with timps, watch the timpanist tuning his drums whilst the music is in progress. He taps the skin, listens very closely with his ear right up against it, and so gets ready for the next passage in the new key, whilst the rest of the orchestra may be playing something quite different.

Another drum to be taken into the orchestra is the side drum, which is an enlargement of the old tabor, with a snare of several gut or coiled wire strings stretched diagonally across it to give the special effect of sonority. In his Fifth Symphony, the Danish composer Carl Nielsen directed the side drummer

Below: a selection of small drums which began to be introduced into Europe from about 1930 onwards by American bands. The ones shown here are of wood, and the skin is held on a wooden or metal frame, the tension of which is controlled by the screws around the edge of the drums. They have a fundamental role in many dance orchestras and jazz bands, and have found their way into the symphony orchestra in the works of Gershwin and Poulenc, for example.

to improvize 'as if at all costs he wants to stop the progress of the orchestra' and he does just that.

Slightly larger than the side drum, and without a snare, is the tenor drum. Finally, the big bass drum is extremely shallow in relation to its diameter and is therefore placed vertically on its side and the player can steady it if necessary as he strikes it. It is not tuneable.

Drumsticks

Before leaving the drum family, a word should be said about drumsticks, for they involve principles fundamental to almost all the percussion instruments. The way in which percussion instruments are struck is most important and obviously more noise is produced when a thing is hit hard rather than gently. However, it is more subtle than that. A very different sound is produced when a cymbal is clashed against another cymbal or when it is slid across another cymbal or hit with a drumstick. The object used to strike the instrument is important. The sound produced varies enormously according to the type of drumstick used to beat a drum. The heads of the sticks may be hard or soft, of felt, wool, wood or even of ivory. In dance bands metal brushes are used to skim the skin and so produce the persistent swishing sound. In one of his works Bartók requires knitting needles to be used for the side drum. From this it should be obvious that the drum is not simply there to produce rhythm or make more noise. It is capable of very subtle and varied effects.

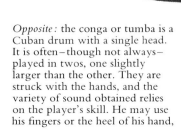

Opposite: the conga or tumba is a Cuban drum with a single head. It is often–though not always–played in twos, one slightly larger than the other. They are struck with the hands, and the variety of sound obtained relies on the player's skill. He may use his fingers or the heel of his hand, the flat palm or the fingers bent. He may play on the centre of the head or near the edge.
Top: a modern bass drum and a snare drum. The purpose of the snare is to vibrate against the head of the drum and give added resonant effects.

Above: a pair of small kettledrums –with a single cowbell–known in France as *timbales créoles*, and therefore having exotic Caribbean associations.

MELODIC PERCUSSION INSTRUMENTS

Xylophones

In essence the xylophone is a very primitive instrument, and is found in many parts of the world. The marimba of Southern Mexico is one of the more popular and sophisticated members of the family and has been used frequently in European music. Perhaps the most advanced of the primitive instruments, however, is the version found in Southeast Asia. The tuned wooden blocks are placed across a resonator, also of wood, which resembles a cradle or trough. The blocks are fastened at one end with a nail, but at the other end they are left free in order to improve the sonority. There are upright nails between the free ends of the blocks, however, to keep them in position. When the wooden blocks were later replaced with metal ones, the xylophone became a metallophone, strictly speaking, because the Greek word, xylon, means wood. This introduction of tuned metal blocks also produced the celesta, which will be looked at in the keyboard section.

In fact the xylophone never became wholly Westernized, despite the fact that it was known in the West from the late fifteenth century. It came into its own much later, via Eastern Europe, and is occasionally used by composers for special

Above: A xylophone from Bonanni's *Gabinetto armonico* (1723), which seems first to have reached Europe in the 16th century, though it was not accepted into the symphony orchestra until the mid-19th century, in an enlarged version, as a melodic percussion instrument.

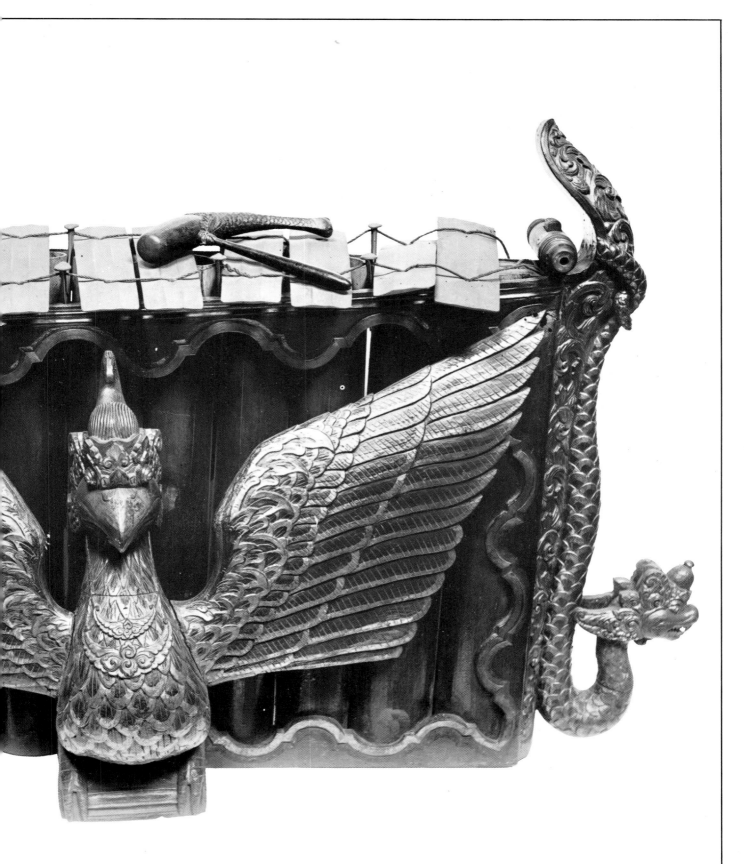

A Javanese xylophone in the
British Museum. The xylophone
ought to be of wood, though
this is by no means the rule,
especially in sophisticated
instruments.

giving all the semitones in the octave-and-a-half from C to F Initially there were only eight bells, then for a while thirteen but to be fully flexible in the modern orchestra eighteen wa found to be the optimum number.

Gongs

Gongs are used in modern symphony orchestras, where the are struck with a bass drumstick, but they are essentially a Oriental instrument. The gong is in the shape of a disc wit its edges turned up, and the most effective place to strike is in the centre, from where the vibrations issue. This is i interesting contrast to the kettledrum, for instance, wher the best place to strike the skin is between the centre and th circumference of the drum itself.

The Chinese had a variety of gongs, and used groups o them together in gong chimes. The Chinese gongs tend t have a central boss–this is certainly true of the larger ones whereas in India there is usually no boss. The gong has neve been particularly current in India, however.

Bells

Bells are of great antiquity and are found in a variety of form throughout the world. They have always had an almos universal association of defence against evil spirits. I Mesopotamia they were used on both clothing and on horse harnesses, though probably for identification rather tha protection in this particular case. In Israel they were used o priestly clothing, though their use was by no means confine to the priesthood, as the scandalized author of *Isaiah III* tells us '. . . the daughters of Zion are haughty, and walk wit stretched forth necks and wanton eyes, walking and mincin as they go, and making a tinkling with their feet.'

In fact the most dire misfortunes were prophesied as result of the behaviour of the haughty ladies:
'In that day the Lord will take away the bravery of thei tinkling ornaments about their feet, and their cauls, and thei round tires like the moon,
The chains, and the bracelets, and the mufflers,
The bonnets, and the ornaments of the legs, and the head bands, and the tablets, and the earrings,
The rings, and nose jewels,
The changeable suits of apparel, and the mantles, an the whimples, and the crisping pins,
The glasses, and the fine linen, and the hoods, and the vails.

Fashion leads people into curious byways, but beware whe bells are the next 'in' thing, particularly round the ankle.

Some magnificent bells were made in China, where the were generally of two kinds: those with internal clappers and those with external striking devices. A curious feature c Chinese bells was their oblong cross-section, also found i ancient Egypt and Ireland, and in Swiss cow-bells. Th

effects. It is often associated with skeletons in music, and a famous film version of *Treasure Island* used it as Ben Gunn's motif in the score.

Vibraphone

A special kind of xylophone deserves mention here because it depends for its effect on an electric, or occasionally clockwork, mechanism and from this point of view it is one of the first musical instruments, along with the Ondes Martenot, to bridge the gap between the pre-electric and the post-electric era. It is also one of the most recent instruments to be accepted in serious music. The vibraphone was invented in America in the 1920s. It follows the basic structure of the more advanced xylophones, that is a series of tuned metal bars given added resonance when struck by the placing of metal resonating tubes under each bar. The innovatory feature of the vibraphone, however, is that the tops of the resonating tubes may be opened and closed by means of a fan which is electrically, or occasionally clockwork, controlled. The effect of the fan is to give the shimmering vibrato effect which is so characteristic of the vibraphone. The speed of the fans can be regulated, and therefore the speed of the vibrato. Also, the effect can be stopped or damped very quickly, which gives the instrument great efficiency and flexibility.

Tubular Bells

These are not bells as we normally tend to think of them, but are metal tubes suspended from a rack, and graded according to pitch, so that when struck with a hammer they sound like bells. Nowadays there are usually eighteen bells in a set,

The Turkish Crescent or Jingling Johnny was known in Central Europe for some two or three centuries before it spread to the rest of the Continent after 1800. *Opposite*: this beautifully carved Benin ivory double bell with its striker comes from Africa and is now in the British Museum.

by their familiar voices, now called upon the citizens to mourn and now to rejoice, now warned them of danger, now exhorted them to piety. They were known by their names, big Jacqueline, or the bell Roland. Every one knew the difference in meaning of the various ways of ringing. However continuous the ringing of the bells, people would seem not to have become blunted to the effect of their sound'.

Whatever their original significance, from an anthropological point of view, bells in Western Europe have always had a more practical and less ritualistic application.

In one form, however, the West produced something original in bells and this was the carillon. Sets of bells had been used in monasteries from the ninth century onwards. It was a particular development of the flat lands of Northern France and present-day Belgium and Holland that immensely high belfries were built, and carillons, connected to a clock or a clockwork mechanism, were installed in them. The mechanism could be arranged in such a way that the bells were played in a special sequence, which gradually became more and more elaborate, so that whole tunes could be played. A cylinder with projecting pegs activated the hammers as it rotated, very much on the lines of the musical box. From the rotating cylinder it was a relatively short step to a keyboard. Eventually it was discovered that bronze blocks gave much the same effect as bells, and took up much less space and time, and so the glockenspiel was born. Another offshoot is a carillon consisting of specially prepared pieces of piano wire struck with hammers from a short manual or keyboard. When amplified electronically, the effect is very like the real thing, though disquieting to the purist.

Before leaving the subject of bells, a distinction should be made between the carillon and the habit of ringing bells by hand. The carillon essentially plays tunes and is controlled by a machine or a player. Change-ringing, on the other hand, consists of a team of ringers who use a variety of permutations in the order of playing, starting from a chosen sequence and eventually returning to that sequence. Another difference is that a carillon strikes the stationary bells, but ringing involves swinging the bell completely over.

Jingling Johnny and Triangle

A rather rare instrument which incorporates bells is the Jingling Johnny or Turkish Crescent. As the name suggests, it was introduced into Europe from Turkey, and makes an extremely decorative addition to the military band, even if the sound is less of an acoustic embellishment. Jingles were also used on triangles at one time, though the practice was abandoned towards the end of the eighteenth century or early in the nineteenth. The triangle is a delightful instrument for heightening orchestration. Beethoven used it in the Ninth Symphony to effect, but it is put to more subtle use in the hands of later and more colourful orchestrators such as Brahms. However, these last two instruments really belong to the last group of percussion instruments, which we shall now consider.

elliptical and circular cross-sections were much later developments. Some Chinese bells were set on the ground on a cushion or similar suitable rest, open side uppermost, and then struck on the edge. It is the edge of a bell which is resonantly live. In China bells were also used in chimes.

The two sorts of bells, with and without a clapper, were found in medieval Europe, but bells never played quite the same role in European life that they did in the East, despite Johann Huizinga's brilliant evocation at the beginning of his classic study, *The Waning of the Middle Ages*:

'One sound rose ceaselessly above the noises of busy life and lifted all things unto a sphere of order and serenity: the sound of bells. The bells were in daily life like good spirits, which

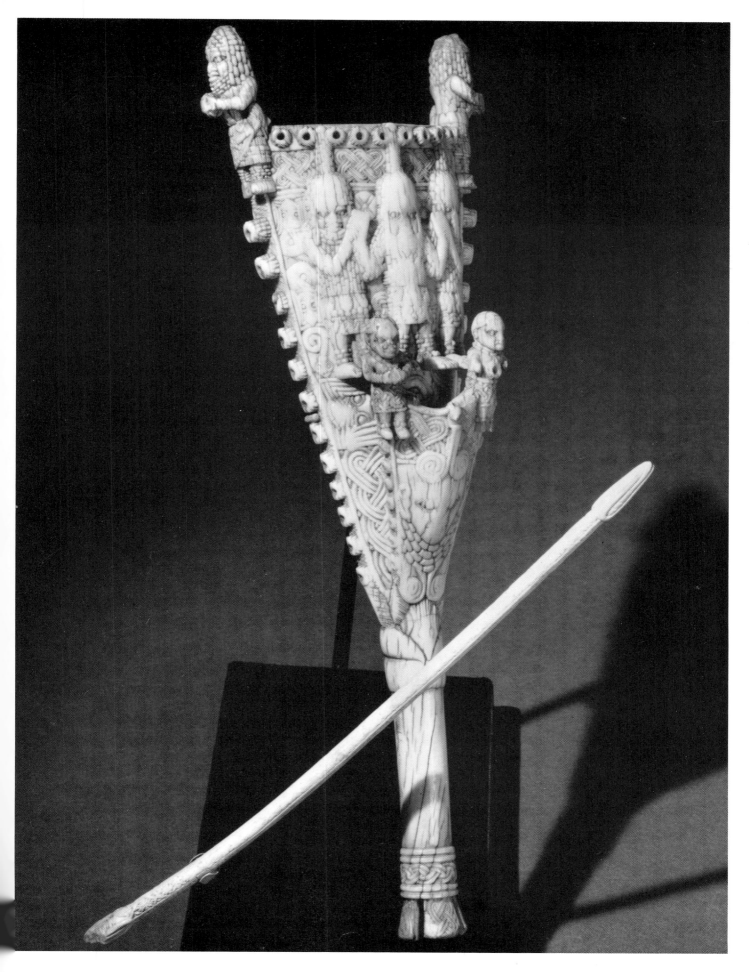

NON-MELODIC PERCUSSION INSTRUMENTS

Rattles

In general rattles are made of several sounding pieces which, when shaken together, strike each other and so give out a sound. A baby's rattle is an obvious example, and a football rattle, though slightly more sophisticated, still works on the same principle, because although the sounding pieces are fixed, they are propelled against each other, or another piece of wood, by the turning of a rachet connected to, or part of, the handle.

In some of the very simple primitive forms, nutshells, seeds, teeth or puffin beaks are simply strung together. Alternatively, these objects or small stones may be put into a gourd or, where there are no gourds available, basketry, pottery or metal shapes. These were the forerunners of the lavishly produced instruments which are now such a characteristic feature of Latin American orchestras. In a much more simple form they have been found in many parts of the world as children's toys, particularly in Mesopotamia and Central America, in the shape of animals or with the pie-crust pattern edge.

Sistrum

The sistrum is a very special kind of rattle. It was usually a U-shaped object closed at the bottom end with a cross-bar to which a handle was attached. However, some of the examples which have survived from the Middle East had handles at the opposite end, at the top of the curve of the U. More crossbars ran from side to side of the uprights of the U, but were loose so that they would rattle against the frame. Originally the sistrum was the attribute of the Egyptian goddess Isis, and when her cult was taken over by the Romans, the sistrum might have been found virtually anywhere in the Roman Empire. Sometimes, to increase the noise, discs were hung on the cross-bars. The sistrum was not exclusively associated with the cult of Isis, however, and examples have been found in the Middle East which are indigenous, and they are still used in the Coptic Christian Church in Ethiopia.

Clappers

Clappers are another primitive percussion instrument. They obviously had a very practical use in protecting crops or

Below: one of Luca della Robbia's
marble reliefs made around 1430
for the *cantoria* or singers' gallery
in Florence Cathedral and now in
the Cathedral museum. The
cymbals are here being played in
the horizontal position.
Opposite: a mounted German
kettledrummer from a 16th-
century engraving in the library
of the Musée des Arts Decoratifs,
Paris. The fact that the drum is
covered may mean that it was
used in a funeral procession.

Æneator

83

Opposite: a page from the late 14th-century King Wenceslas Bible in the Austrian National Library, Vienna (Codex 2759, folio 69 verso). The women in procession carry handbells and two small drums beaten with sticks.

Below: a mosaic from Pompeii by Dioscorides of Samos, now in the National Museum, Naples. It dates from the 1st century BC and shows Roman street musicians with a double aulos, small cymbals and a frame drum.

providing rhythm for the treading of grapes. In view of the close connections between nature and religion in early societies, it was only a short step to the inclusion of clappers and similar instruments as an integral part of cult worship. Instruments of this sort have survived from Egypt and Mesopotamia, and also from Carthage, which throws an interesting light on the origin of the castanet. The Mediterranean coast of Spain and the Balearic Islands were at one time flourishing Carthaginian colonies. The clappers tended to be played exclusively by women, as they were in Greece and Rome.

In Oriental music, particularly that of China and Southeast Asia, clappers have always had a part to play. In the West, however, they inevitably retained their original practical function. In the Middle Ages, for example, lepers carried clappers to warn people off. Occasionally, however, they are called for today in the percussion section of a modern orchestra, since a single stroke of a clapper gives a sound like a crack of a whip and occasionally the sound of the anvil is called for as well. Wood blocks are also used in the percussion section of the orchestra, though the sound is of a different nature. One of the more fascinating pieces of modern music for the vividness with which it handles the percussion effects is Sir William Walton's oratorio *Belshazzar's Feast*, which revels in the opportunities to distinguish between gold and silver, wood and iron in one part of the text.

Cymbals

Of the non-melodic instruments of percussion, the cymbals are probably the most exciting when in action. Cymbals existed in two forms in Mesopotamia. The small, funnel-shaped variety were gently struck together whilst held in a horizontal position. A charming temple frieze from Thailand shows how far this kind of cymbal travelled. Fragments in the author's possession show a group of temple musicians amongst whom are drummers, a woman with a tiny gong and embellished drumstick head, and another woman playing small, funnel-shaped cymbals in the horizontal position.

The slightly larger variety of cymbal was held vertically and clashed together, as in the modern symphony orchestra. Some ancient Egyptian cymbals which have survived are large, whereas others are quite small, and some on sticks are apparently cymbals or clappers, and as such akin to castanets. One sees in this case just how closely the three are related.

Ancient China had cymbals, as did India, and there was an old tradition that they were taken to China from India. What is more likely is that they were taken to both countries by the Huns, for it was also ultimately from the Huns, via Turkey, that cymbals came to Europe. Initially in Europe they had a purely military function, but gradually they found their way into orchestral music too. Today their most frequent use is in the rhythm section of the dance band and pop group. It is curious that in spite of attempts to find new textures in pop music, no one seems to have explored further the possiblities of the percussion section. Generally speaking there are only three small drums, two side drums and a tenor, and a bass drum which is struck with a pedal-operated stick. The cymbals are suspended horizontally, either singly or in pairs, and can also be operated by pedal.

Unfortunately the other instruments are generally amplified to such a pitch, and this is particularly true of pop groups, that anything but the most penetrating timbre is condemned to obscurity or simply used to boost the general output of decibels. It may not be too fanciful to suppose that in the future a reaction will set in, and a renewed interest in individual and distinctive timbres will overtake the pop scene but at a much less frenetic dynamic than at present.

A set of three cymbals (*left*) as used widely today.

An Indian vina from Bonanni's *Gabinetto armonico*, though in fact he took it from Mersenne's *Harmonie universelle* of 1636–7. The stick body has two gourd resonators, movable frets and five strings, which are plucked by the thumbs and fingertips with metal plectra. However, since Mersenne showed only one string, and simply marked the places for the pegs for the other four strings, the engraver mistakenly thought that it was a type of single-stringed percussion instrument played with sticks.

Surprisingly, perhaps, the realm of non-melodic percussion instruments is one where the highly sophisticated modern symphony orchestra most readily meets the long traditions of folk and ethnic music, represented here by an 8th-century Mayan wall painting in which can be seen drums and rattles. Nevertheless, in an age when the mainstream of Western Classical music is in considerable disarray, the continuing existence of living folk traditions such as those of Central and South America, with their very distinctive rhythms and timbres, provides a refreshing and hopeful source of pleasure and inspiration, as well as proof of enormous resilience to external pressures in a world that is all too prone to exploit ethnic diversity for its own ends.

Children making Music, 1629, by the Flemish artist Jan Molenaer, in the National Gallery, London. At this time the violin had scarcely become a socially acceptable instrument, and in this picture is accompanied by two rather crude percussion instruments, namely a friction drum – which is nothing more than a skin fixed over a suitable pot or jug with a stick passing through it – and a metal helmet struck with a pair of spoons. The sounds produced can scarcely have been very melodious.

Keyboard Instruments

The musical personality of a pianist directly affects the interpretation of a composer's work, and the same piece of music may sound completely different when performed by such contrasting artists as the late Sir Clifford Curzon (left) and the Russian Emil Gilels (right). Not only basic technique, but touch, handling of tempi and emotional response to the music determine the nature of performances.

Curzon's commitment to the music – especially that of Mozart – proclaimed itself in unmistakable emotional terms. Gilels' readings, however, though no less profound, are performed in an almost impassive trance. The refusal to play encores implicitly affirms that all available physical, intellectual and emotional resources have been expended on the chosen programme.

Keyboard instruments are perhaps the most accessible, and at the same time the most neglected, as far as a great many people are concerned. Towards the end of the last century there were few households without a piano of some sort, and the very expression 'cottage' piano testifies to their popularity. Countless children set out regularly, with the best will in the world, for their weekly piano lesson, and then fall by the wayside. But pianos are not the only keyboard instruments. There are in fact two main kinds – stringed and wind :-

Right: the harpsichord by Jan Ruckers, Antwerp 1634, at Ham House, near Richmond, Surrey. This instrument was restored by Arnold Dolmetsch in 1894, which may be the date of the pedals for changing the stops. The natural keys are of ivory with ebony moulded fronts and the accidentals are of ebony. It is thought that the keys and the three early stop handles of turned brass are 18th-century English work, and the instrument may have been restored at that time.

Below: this spinet, usually known as Queen Elizabeth's Virginals, is probably a late 16th-century instrument of Italian construction. It is built of cypress wood, and on a panel to the left of the keyboard is the coat-of-arms borne by English monarchs from Henry IV to Elizabeth I. On the right is the badge of Anne Boleyn and her daughter, Queen Elizabeth. There is another instrument in Leipzig University Museum made by Benedetto Floriani in 1571 which is remarkably like this instrument.

Left: a positive organ, Renaissance harp and large five-stringed fiddle on a panel of the Ghent Polyptych by Jan van Eyck in the Cathedral of St Bavon. In relation to the size of the organ and the magnificent rendering of the metal pipes, the manual or keyboard appears remarkably insignificant. In view of its earlier pagan associations, however, the very acceptance of the organ by the Christian church was a remarkable phenomenon.

STRINGED KEYBOARD INSTRUMENTS

These instruments may be treated in the same way as we treated the non-keyboard stringed instruments, namely by the way they are sounded. There is really only one bowed keyboard stringed instrument, however, and that is the hurdy gurdy, which was included with the non-keyboard section because in shape, evolution and general principle it belongs there. The whole accent in keyboard instruments is on the facilities provided by the striking and, to a lesser degree, the plucking action operated by a key from a manual or keyboard. The hurdy gurdy's essential characteristic is not a direct result of its keyboard nature, so much as its stringed nature. In other words, there is a fundamental similarity amongst keyboard instruments, which is stronger than the various means of producing sound. Since the plucked stringed keyboard instruments have remained at the same stage of evolution for some time now, in fact some would maintain that they visibly regressed in the eighteenth century as they struggled to survive, we will consider them first.

Harpsichords and Spinets

These are the chief representatives of the plucked keyboard instruments. The common principle is that of a small, upright piece of wood or jack attached to the end of each key, with a quill or leather tongue projecting from the jack. The jacks are not rigidly attached to the keys, but are free-standing and are held in a rack inside the soundboard, which runs the whole length of the box. When a key is depressed the jack rises, the quill plucks the string and then falls back without touching the string a second time.

It would be as well at this point to clear up a question of terminology. A great deal of confusion has been caused by the fact that the terms virginal and spinet were used inconsistently in the past, and therefore two quite distinctive instruments were thought to have been involved. In fact the word virginal or virginals was widely used in England until well into the seventeenth century to cover all keyboard instruments of the plucked kind, and in some cases the clavichord, a struck instrument, as well. An inventory of Henry VIII for 1547 mentions: 'Twoo faire paire of newe long Virginalles made harpe fasshion'. This, incidentally, disproves the theory frequently advanced in the past that virginals were so named for Queen Elizabeth I, the Virgin Queen, since she was not born until 1533, and the virginal was already established by the time her father's inventory was drawn up in 1547.

More practical information is to be drawn from the title of such collections as The Fitzwilliam Virginal Book. Here the term virginal is evidently used in a very wide sense, and in the second volume of his *Syntagma Musicum* (1614–19), Michael Praetorius says under the section spinetta: 'In England all these instruments, be they large or small, are called *Virginall*'. Further evidence comes from a most telling quotation from Samuel Pepys's diary for 4 April 1668, in which he says: '. . . called upon one Hayward, that makes virginalls, and did there like of a little espinette, and will have him finish it for me; for I had a mind to a small harpsichon, but this takes up less room . . .'.

It becomes clear, therefore, that virginals was a generic term. The word spinet (Pepys's espinette) was used to designate the wing-shaped or polygonal instrument known in France as *épinette* and in Italy as *spinetta*. Two particular features, however, distinguish the Italian products, and these characteristics are also shared by the Italian harpsichords. First of all the instruments were nearly always of cypress wood, with a soundboard of cypress or cedar wood and secondly, in view of their fragile nature, they nearly always had an outer case, which might be decorated in a variety of ways.

There was a marked contrast between the spinets produced in Italy, and those in the Low Countries. Flemish spinets were normally of pinewood, and rectangular in form. One town, Antwerp, concentrated the instrument-building business, and was a centre of export for the world. Towards the end of the fifteenth century it rapidly took over from Bruges as the artistic centre of the Low Countries. In Antwerp one family

virtually re-built in Paris during the eighteenth century. This was not a matter of wanton destruction. On the contrary, the tone of the Ruckers instruments was highly prized, and it was in an attempt to preserve and enlarge the tonal quality that the Parisian builders set about their work.

The Russell Collection in Edinburgh has three Ruckers instruments, as has the Victoria and Albert Museum in London. Two of the Edinburgh instruments are two-manual transposing instruments. The idea of the transposing instrument was fairly common before the standardization of pitch, and it enabled one harpsichord to be used with different instruments at different pitch, since it was obviously not practical to retune a harpsichord every time a different pitch was encountered.

The earlier instrument in Edinburgh is by Andries Ruckers, the Elder, and is dated 1608. Unfortunately it has gone through many vicissitudes. First of all it was rebuilt with two manuals at the same pitch and then in the 18th century it was rebuilt as a pianoforte, and at that time the upper manual was removed. It was only some forty years ago that it was restored as a harpsichord and the second manual refitted. Until 1953, however, when it underwent a further restoration, the lower manual had been the original Ruckers manufacture. It is now displayed separately in the collection.

Opposite: A clavicytherium from Bonanni's *Gabinetto armonico* (1723). The Italian name – *cembalo verticale* – tells us that its strings run vertically, at right angles to the keyboard. Although it took up less space than a horizontal instrument, the technical problems created for the action were a serious disadvantage for the clavicytherium.
Above: A Ruckers harpsichord with a single manual. It is now in the Gemeentemuseum in The Hague.
Right: *Parthenia*, published in London in 1611, was the first collection engraved for keyboard instruments. It contained works by Byrd, Bull and Gibbons.

in particular – the Ruckers – made themselves world-famous as instrument makers. In the late seventeenth and early eighteenth centuries, however, the initiative passed to France, though both Germany and England produced excellent instrument makers, and in eighteenth-century England the spinet was almost as common as the upright piano used to be in English homes in more recent times.

The Ruckers family are vitally important in the history of the harpsichord and virginal, because they influenced every national school of harpsichord making apart from those of Italy and Spain.

Hans Ruckers, the founder of the dynasty, was born in Malines around the middle of the sixteenth century and by the 1570s he was working in Antwerp. Two of his sons, Jan and Andries (or Andreas), joined him in the business, as did Andries's son, also called Andries. There are about 140 or 150 recorded instruments from the workshops which are known to have survived, but many more must have been in existence, and may still survive. Unfortunately many of them were

But it is the 1638 Jan Ruckers harpsichord which is the most fascinating, because it is a unique surviving example of a two-manual transposing instrument which has never been tampered with. The inner surfaces are still lined with the original Ruckers papers. This is also true of the Jan Ruckers instrument dating from 1634 which is at Ham House, Richmond-upon-Thames, Surrey (though under the administration of the Victoria and Albert Museum, and included in its catalogue as a result). However, this is less interesting from a musical point of view.

Of the two other instruments in the Victoria and Albert Museum made by the Ruckers Family, one belonged to King George III, but was sold when Queen Charlotte received a new Kirkman instrument in 1766, and the other is reputed to have belonged to Handel. The evidence for this is not conclusive, however, and one can only regard it as a romantic association.

The larger instrument which we know as the harpsichord (Pepys's 'harpsichon') is in French *clavecin* and in Italian, *clavicembalo*. In fact the early harpsichords were quite modest instruments. The earliest authentically dated harpsichord is an Italian specimen of 1521 in the Victoria and Albert Museum, London. It has one manual or keyboard, and one set of strings, with a fairly low sound, which is equivalent to the sound emitted by an eight-foot organ stop. We saw in the lute family of stringed instruments how a single set of strings might be employed, and how double strings known as courses might be contemplated for improving the tone of the instrument. By the end of the sixteenth century, double courses of strings were common on harpsichords, but they were higher in pitch, being equivalent to a four-foot organ stop. This designation of the pitch of harpsichords in terms of organ pipes may well confuse a person who is not aware of what it stands for. It does not imply that there are harpsichords with organ pipes, though there was an instrument known as the claviorgan in existence at one time.

The addition of a second manual or keyboard to the harpsichord began to give even greater possibilities for its development, and a wider tonal variety was produced by the introduction of two effects, that of the harp—a slide with small pads of buff leather which muted the strings and gave a plucked effect rather like a violin played *pizzicato*—and that of the lute—a second set of jacks which plucked the strings much closer to the wrest plank, and therefore gave a tonal quality akin to that of the lute. These two effects were known as stops because they were controlled by an action very similar to that used for the stops on an organ. Although the idea is similar—that of the introduction of tonal variety—in both instruments, there is obviously no further parallel, because one is a stringed and the other a wind instrument. Nevertheless it remains confusing for the uninitiated to hear the terms stops, manual and feet (for pitch) used in connection

with both organ and harpsichord. One can only stress that the problem is basically one of semantics.

Some harpsichords had their strings running vertically, and they were then known as *clavicytheria* (*-ium* in the singular). This had the advantage of taking up less space and of projecting the sound directly at the listener. However, since the jacks could not fall back of their own accord in this position, but had to be pulled back, a much more complicated mechanism was required and the instrument was consequently not very popular.

Eventually, as the pianoforte made its appearance in the second half of the eighteenth century, two more effects were added to the harpsichord in a desperate bid to retain the popularity of the instrument. One was a purely mechanical device which allowed the player to change the stops and combinations of effects by pedal, so that the hands were left free for the keyboard. Another was the introduction of a swell box, as on organs, whereby the opening and closing of a shutter increased or decreased the volume. By this time, however, the battle had already been lost to the pianoforte, and the golden age of the harpsichord was over. Harpsichords continued to be made in Paris and London into the early years of the nineteenth century, and in Germany and Scandinavia even later.

The rapid decline in the supremacy of the harpsichord is vividly demonstrated by two instruments which are also housed in the Russell Collection in Edinburgh. The first is a two-manual harpsichord by Jacob Kirkman or Kirckman, dating from 1773, number 16 in the collection. Kirkman was born near Strasbourg in 1710, and came to England as a young man of twenty or so. He worked for a Flemish *émigré* called Hermann Tabel, and at Tabel's death married his widow. Tabel is an important figure in the history of the keyboard tradition in the Western world, because he learnt his trade in Antwerp and so handed on to Kirkman a long tradition of craftsmanship. Another of his pupils was Burkat Shudi, who founded the house of Broadwood. Tabel is thus a vital link between the world of the harpsichord and spinet and the modern pianoforte. Kirkman's firm eventually included his nephew and great-nephew, and more than one hundred of their harpsichords survive.

The Edinburgh instrument is a typical example of an English harpsichord at the height of its development. The case is of mahogany inlaid with fine bands of lighter wood, and it has its original stand. The natural keys are of ivory and the accidentals—or sharps and flats—are of ebony. It has a lute stop and a harp stop, together with a machine stop. The idea of the machine stop is rather like the idea of pistons on a pipe organ. By using two pedals in a variety of combinations the player is able to alter the tonal effects without taking his hands off the manuals.

It is fascinating to compare the instrument just described with one built only twenty years later, number 19 in the collection. This is a Broadwood harpsichord, in fact it bears the last recorded number and date of a Broadwood harpsichord, and is the only instrument inscribed by Broadwood alone.

Opposite: A Girl playing a Clavichord by Jan van Hemessen, 1534, now in the Worcester Art Museum, Massachusetts. The inherent delicacy of the clavichord is admirably suggested in this picture.

The harpsichord by Jerome of Bologna, made in Rome in 1521, in the Victoria and Albert Museum, London. The nameboard appears genuine, as well as the inscription on it, so there is no reason to doubt that this is at present the oldest instrument of its kind known in the world. The outer case, from which the harpsichord may be removed, dates from the 17th century. Its relationship to the instrument itself may be clearly seen in the illustration below.

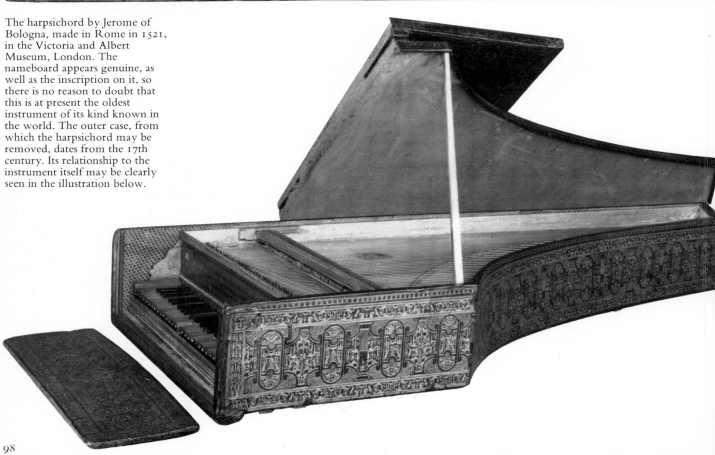

Below: a harpsichord made by Giovanni Baffo in Venice in 1574, and restored at the Victoria and Albert Museum in 1964, when the gilt arabesques were discovered on the outside of the case. The instrument was once longer, since the pattern on the inside of the lid is cut short.

Bottom: an Italian octave spinet from about 1600 in the Victoria and Albert Museum. Charles Burney, who toured Italy in 1770, was very scathing about this kind of instrument.

An English spinet made by John Player in London in the second half of the 17th century. It seems that the stand is the original. The natural keys are of ebony and the accidentals of ivory. The aerial view vividly emphasises the difference between the longest and shortest string length.

A 16th-century clavichord in the museum of the Paris Conservatoire. Though larger than the instrument shown on p. 96, the intimate nature of the clavichord is still evident here.

Broadwood was born in Berwickshire in 1732 and, as Kirkman had done before him, he went to London in his early twenties. By 1761 he was working for Burkat Shudi, and from 1770 the instruments they produced were signed jointly Shudi and Broadwood. In 1795 the firm took the name of Broadwood. From 1773 Broadwood built square pianos, and from 1781 grand pianos as well. The harpsichord of 1793 in the Russell Collection is therefore something of a survival from antiquity, rather in the nature of a prehistoric monster found in some remote region. And in the way that some prehistoric monsters had huge bodies and tiny heads, it is amusing to see that, for all its considerable bulk, the Broadwood harpsichord has only a tiny, single manual. The impression of bulk is increased by the opening of the shutters of the Venetian swell, and it is this feature which really sets the seal on its decadence. When the swell is opened by depressing the right-hand pedal beneath the keyboard, the slats of the swell–which run the length of the instrument–rise like so many mouths.

Clavichords

The clavichord evolved from the medieval monochord. However, it was presumably a monochord with several strings, and in fact Johannes de Muris, in his *Musica speculativa* of 1323, mentions a monochord with nineteen strings. Like the monochord, the clavichord is basically a simple instrument. It is first recorded at the beginning of the fifteenth century, and the oldest surviving specimen, in the Metropolitan Museum, New York, is dated 1537, though it is more than likely that there were earlier instruments which have perished or been incorporated into later instruments.

In element the clavichord consists of a shallow box with strings running from left to right. At the left they are secured by hitch pins. At the right they are tuned by pegs screwed into a wrest plank, to which the soundboard is attached. The strings are set in vibration by brass tangents which strike when the keys are depressed. Since the length of the vibrating string in the clavichord does not depend on the overall length of the string, but on the distance between the bridge (on the soundboard) and the tangents, several tangents can produce different notes on the same string, depending on where they are placed along it. Later clavichords had one string–or more usually two–to each key of the keyboard, but the fact that they were larger, more expensive, and took longer to tune, was not in their favour.

By any standards the tone of the clavichord is weak, but by careful control of the pressure of the tangent on the strings, the player has at his disposal a variety of expression which no other stringed keyboard instrument was able to provide until the piano was invented. By a curious paradox, of all the instruments to be revived in recent years the clavichord has probably, from a musical point of view, been least successful. Clavichord enthusiasts will hotly contest this, but when compared with an eighteenth-century instrument a modern clavichord is but a pale shadow from the tonal point of view. A certain amount of harm has been done to the cause of the clavichord by attempting to turn it into a recital instrument. It is hard to see how this can be satisfactorily achieved, except in the most intimate of settings, and to amplify the instrument is the height of bad taste. Moreover amplification makes most modern clavichords sound like guitars.

At the height of its popularity the clavichord probably

had most success in Germany, where the Silbermann family, in the eighteenth century, provided the most distinguished group of makers. Christian Schubert (1739–91) said: 'Who dislikes noise, raging and fuming, whose heart bursts in sweet feelings, neglects both the harpsichord and the piano and chooses the clavichord'.

Chekker

A great deal of discussion has raged around the instrument known as the chekker, which was particularly popular not only in England, but also in Burgundy, France and Spain from the fourteenth to the sixteenth centuries. It seems to have differed from the clavichord in some respects, and also from the spinet (which is of course a plucked instrument), though in other respects it is similar to both these instruments. Kurt Sachs came down in favour of the spinet-type instrument or, to be more exact, said that it was a portative upright harpsichord. What is certain is that the action of the chekker, in a way similar to that of the dulcimer, anticipated the pianoforte, which we shall consider next, by several hundred years.

Pianoforte

It has already been pointed out that the dulcimer and chekker were forerunners of the pianoforte–to give it its full name. Henceforth we can use the more common form piano. There is another instrument which deserves attention, however, before considering the piano proper. A fifteenth-century manuscript in the Bibliothèque Nationale, Paris, describes something called a dulce melos, which appears to have been a stringed keyboard instrument in which the strings were struck from below. When first published in the early nineteenth century, this manuscript seemed to describe the action of the piano. The action of the dulce melos was vertical, however, whereas that of the piano is essentially a rotary or swinging one. Nevertheless, latent elements seemed to have been pointing to the piano, and one day the right person came along to realize those latent elements.

Credit for the invention of the piano is given to Bartolommeo Cristofori, a Florentine harpsichord maker who worked under the patronage of Prince Ferdinand de' Medici. The date of 1709 is the traditional one given for his discovery, though recent research puts the date at least a decade earlier. An inventory of the prince's musical instruments of 1700 specifically mentions an 'arpicembale . . . a new invention', and special mention is also made of dampers and hammers. Cristofori's experiments must therefore have been well advanced at least a year or two prior to the date of this inventory. In Paris, the French harpsichord maker Marius demonstrated instruments with hammers to the Royal Academy in 1716, and in Dresden Gottlieb Schroeter presented similar instruments to the royal court in the following year. In fact it was in Germany, under Gottfried Silbermann (1683–1753), that the piano was really developed, and the square piano came into being, inspired by the rectangular shape of the clavichord, which appears to have been more

Opposite: a clavicytherium or upright harpsichord by Albert Delin dating from the second half of the 18th century, and now in the Gemeentemuseum in The Hague. This instrument never had a great success because it was so much less practical than the horizontal harpsichord, even though it took up less space.

Below: a pianoforte by Bartolommeo Cristofori of Florence, 1720, now in the Crosby Brown Collection of Musical Instruments in the Metropolitan Museum, New York. It is Cristofori, an accomplished harpsichord maker, who is credited with the invention of the pianoforte – in element a mechanized dulcimer.

Ralph Kirkpatrick has been one of the few harpsichordists since the revival of the instrument to make an international career as a soloist on that instrument alone. At the same time, however, his profound knowledge of the harpsichord literature and repertoire has been of enormous help in his study of the works of Domenico Scarlatti (1685–1757), and Kirkpatrick has published what is now the standard catalogue of the composer's keyboard output.

Left: an overstrung upright Pleyel piano, showing clearly the strings, the keyboard and the hammer action of the instrument.
Below: a grand pianoforte by John Broadwood & Sons, London 1883. The case was decorated by Kate Faulkner of William Morris & Co., and it is in its decoration that the interest of the instrument consists. The case is of oak stained green and decorated with birds, fruit and flowers carved in relief and then covered with silver and gilt gesso.

acceptable to German taste. There were some early instruments inspired by the harpsichord, and therefore more akin to the modern grand piano in shape. However, they seem to have taken much longer to become popular.

The first public piano recital in England, if not in the whole world, was given in London in 1768 by Johann Christian, son of Johann Sebastian Bach, on a square piano by Zumpe. Zumpe was a former pupil of Silbermann, who had come to England along with several other German piano makers in 1760 when the Seven Years' War drove them out of their own country. With them the centre of piano making moved to England. The square pianos, in an attempt to give special sound effects, had frequently incorporated the very effects which the harpsichord, in its attempt to survive, was using – harps and lute stops, swell boxes and piano pedals. However, they also introduced effects which have become essential features of the modern grand piano, namely the forte and una corda pedals, by which the keyboard is moved along so that the hammers strike only one wire at a time.

There had been an English piano with a pedal as early as 1782, but John Broadwood's patent for a pedal was not taken out until the following year, on 17 July 1783. Although Broadwood did a great deal to develop the modern piano, it was Sebastian Erard (1752–1831) in Paris who perfected the hammer action, and Alphaeus Babcock in Boston, USA, who produced the first fully cast-iron frame. It was Babcock who also invented overstringing or cross-stringing, though

Steinways in New York really developed the idea. Basically, instead of the strings being kept side by side, the treble and bass strings overlap, so that more strings are concentrated near the centre of the soundboard, and a much more powerful sound is obtained. Also, when the dampers are lifted and the strings are allowed to vibrate more, the number of harmonics obtained is increased. That is why some of the very full or thick chords which occur particularly in early nineteenth-century music sound so dense when played on modern pianos. The composers never envisaged their works being played on such instruments.

The square piano was always very popular in America, and continued to be made there until about 1880. By this time, however, it had been very much influenced by the development of the grand, and was almost as vast and as heavy – as anyone who has ever tried to move one knows.

Alongside the development of the grand it must not be forgotten that experiments were going on with an upright piano, although it was only in about 1800 that the idea of the modern upright, with the strings above and below the keyboard, came into being. After all, there had been an upright harpsichord. Some of the early upright pianos were in the shape of a pyramid, and one was known as the giraffe. Another reproduced the shape of the lyre. One extraordinary model in the Victoria and Albert Museum, London, looks like a harp backed by the bodies of three 'cellos, and rejoices in the name of euphonicon.

A grand piano seen from across the keyboard, which makes an interesting comparison with the top illustration opposite. The upright piano is virtually the grand piano on its side with the pegs at the top, and the keyboard at an angle of ninety degrees to the strings, instead of being in the same plane, as on the grand. The dampers and hammers then change sides on the strings.

Below: a grand pianoforte by William Stoddart, made in London round about 1825. The exterior of the case is decorated with rosewood veneering on mahogany with brass stringing. Inside, the case has satinwood veneer with ebony stringing. Unfortunately, the original stringing of this piano has been lost, but there are sufficient indications to show what it once was.

Opposite: a modern Steinway grand piano. It seems hard to imagine that much will ever be done to improve these magnificent instruments. Most of the innovations in the grand piano were made during the life of Liszt (1811–86), and subsequent generations have built on them.

Left: A chamber or 'positive' organ from Bonanni's *Gabinetto armonico* (1723). This kind of instrument would have had wood and open metal pipes only, thus being distinguished more for the purity and gentleness of its tone than for its ability to produce a large amount of sound. Indeed, the term chamber organ implies a more intimate character, and it might be used for both solo work and accompaniment.

One slide governed several pipes, which all sounded together when the slides were pulled out and the wind let into them. In some respects the early pneumatic organs were more primitive than the hydraulic ones, for at least the hydraulos had a steady wind pressure and possibly a stop action to control the sounding of the pipes. The sound of the Winchester organ was probably very uneven and intermittent.

However, the pneumatic organ began to develop after AD 1000. Levers were introduced to replace the slides, and they were organized as a primitive keyboard. Some of the levers were worked directly by the fingers. Others had a system rather like the keys of the modern typewriter, which transferred the pressure to the levers. Then gradually, during the twelfth and thirteenth centuries, the number of keys and ranks of pipes was augmented. They were provided with semitones, and a second manual was introduced so that not all the pipes needed to be sounded.

Possibly the greatest period of development for the organ was from 1400 to 1600. The idea of pedals—really a keyboard played with the feet—was introduced at the beginning of this period, and the method of handling the keys and levers (known as the action) was improved, with the result that the keyboard and the keys themselves could be much smaller. But the most interesting feature from the sound point of view was the changes introduced into the pipes. The earlier organs had several ranks of pipes responding to each lever, tuned in unison, at the fifth (five notes), the octave (eight notes) and the twelfth, and so on. This gave each note rich harmonics, even if the effect was occasionally somewhat strident. But they were all the same tonal effect. The effect is still available on modern organs, but the great innovation at this time, and the great feature of organ playing today, was the practice of adding individual stops, or groups of pipes with very different tonal effects. Briefly, a stop is a set of pipes imitating the timbre of a wind instrument, with a distinctive sound against the diapasons or principals, which usually form the mixture. The name stop is given to the individual sets of pipe because they could be shut off or brought into action by a slide or stop, and from this the usage was extended to the whole set of pipes.

The flute was the earliest solo stop. By the end of the fifteenth century stopped wood and metal pipes were in use as well as reed pipes and narrow, open metal pipes. It may come as a surprise to some people to learn that the tremulant somehow regarded as a vulgar effect at present, though effective when used with discretion, also dates from this time. In open pipes, as the name suggests, the top of the pipes is left open, whether they be of metal or wood. Stopped pipes which are only made of wood, have what is like a plug inserted into the top. This makes the sound much softer, rather like

WIND KEYBOARD INSTRUMENTS

The Organ

The organ is the most complicated and largest musical instrument operated by one person. It is now almost exclusively connected with churches, but was once a very secular instrument. Its invention was attributed to Ktesibios in the second half of the third century BC in Alexandria. Its Greek name, hydraulos, indicates that the wind pressure was supplied by water compression. The penetrating sound was particularly suited to the Roman circus.

It is not clear at what point a purely pneumatic organ was developed, though there are indications that Byzantium was an early centre of organ building, and that the pneumatic organ was known there in the late fourth or fifth centuries AD. From there envoys went to France and Germany with organs as gifts to Pippin the Short and Charlemagne in the eighth and ninth centuries, and in the tenth century a famous organ was built at Winchester in England. The player of the early organ had to have a great deal of strength, since he had to push and pull the slides which connected the individual pipes. Not for nothing was he known as pulsator.

A French chamber organ dating from the first half of the 17th century, now in the Instruments Museum of the Brussels Conservatoire. As the name implies, a chamber organ was usually envisaged for use in a private apartment, which meant that it would have only limited keyboard compass and limited tonal quality. Moreover, the design of the case would be of considerable importance. When the painted doors were closed, this instrument would look like a cabinet, and give little or no indication of its real purpose, unless the bellows or blowing mechanism were to be visible from a different viewpoint.

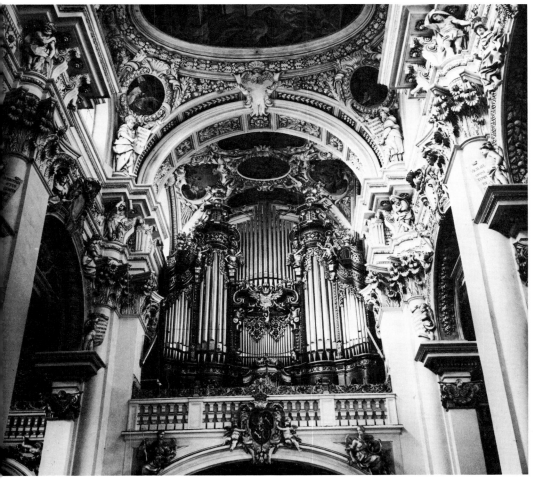

The organ in the Baroque church at Passau in Austria. Since articulation was one of the essential characteristics of the Baroque period in music, it was almost inevitable that the organ should expand in response to this aim, for with its pedal board and variety of manuals or keyboards, the organ already had more possibilities for articulation in performance than any other instrument of its day. To this was added the enormous range of tonal variety provided by the stops, each one controlling a particular set of pipes to give either solo effects or a mixture of timbres. Moreover these timbres might be used in a number of possible combinations with the pedals and/or the other manuals, so that in the hands of an imaginative and inventive executant, the organ became truly the king of instruments.

a mute in a brass instrument. A reed has, as the name suggests, a reed in the pipe which beats in the airstream. In the flue pipe, however, there is simply a lip or hole in the wall of the pipe, with a projection inside, just below the hole. The airstream encounters the projection and the sound is emitted.

During the period of the decline of the harpsichord and the rise of the piano, the organ also benefited from the experiments with swell boxes, and in fact the final effect of this in the organ is to have one manual controlling what is virtually a complete, smaller organ enclosed in a box with shutters to be opened or closed at will, to swell or diminish the sound. The same idea of one manual controlling one section of the organ can be used to explain the reason for as many as four, or even five manuals on some of the larger organs. These are Choir, Swell, Great and Solo with sometimes an Echo organ. The manuals can be coupled together and in this way elements from other parts of the organ used in a variety of permutations and combinations.

In the same way the manuals can be coupled to the pedal organ, which is virtually another manual played with the feet, as has already been suggested. This pedalboard should not be confused with the pedal which controls the Swell, or the pedals which bring out combinations of stops, thus allowing the organist to arrange his effects beforehand, and instead of having to draw them out individually he can add several at once. An additional aid for this is the thumb pistons under the front of the keys of each manual. If an organist is to give a recital, he can alter the stops allocated to each piston. This has resulted in some odd effects when visiting organists have given recitals and the resident organist has had to use his instrument before the pistons have been altered back.

A whole book could be devoted to the endless variety of organ stops–particularly since modern organ builders seem to compete with each other in giving deliberately obscure names to what is basically the same stop. Then there is the question of the various types of action available today, which is really beyond the scope of this book. Until fairly recently tracker action (basically a mechanical means of transferring the touch on the keys to make the pipes sound) was regarded as antiquated, and was replaced by electric action. Now tracker action seems to be returning to popularity once more. Certainly the introduction of electric action has made it possible for the console or playing part of the organ to be set apart from the pipes. This is obviously of benefit to the organist, who is able to hear what effects he is obtaining, particularly when he is accompanying singers, who might be a long way away from the organ, especially in cathedrals and

An illustration from the Cambridge Psalter in Trinity College Library, Cambridge (MS. B 18 folio 1), dating from the 12th century. This organ was taken from the 9th-century Utrecht Psalter, which in turn drew its inspiration from an early Byzantine organ. There seem to be remarkably few pipes in relation to the amount of work being put into blowing the bellows, and the fact that two people appear to be required to play the instrument.

large churches. Judging time lag in heavily resonant building is something to which organists have to adjust. A relayed be by an assistant or a looking-glass perched at a crazy angle a two of the most frequently encountered expedients, thoug none can have been more frustrating to organist and singe alike than the extraordinary wooden hand, activated fro behind, which still points out from the choir screen at Rip Cathedral.

Portative organs are small organs which may be carrie around easily–particularly in processions. Until the end the sixteenth century they were frequently used in the larg churches. They should not be confused with the reg however, which was essentially only a reed organ to beg with–and as such a forerunner of the harmonium–thoug later, flue pipes were added. At this point, however, th distinction between regal and portative organ virtuall disappears.

A double manual regal in Kremsmunster Abbey. Originally the regal consisted of reed pipes only when it was invented during the second half of the 15th century. Later the reed pipes were confined to the regal stop, and flue pipes were added. When reed pipes were then added to a positive organ such as that on p. 93, the basic distinction between the regal and the positive organ tended to disappear.

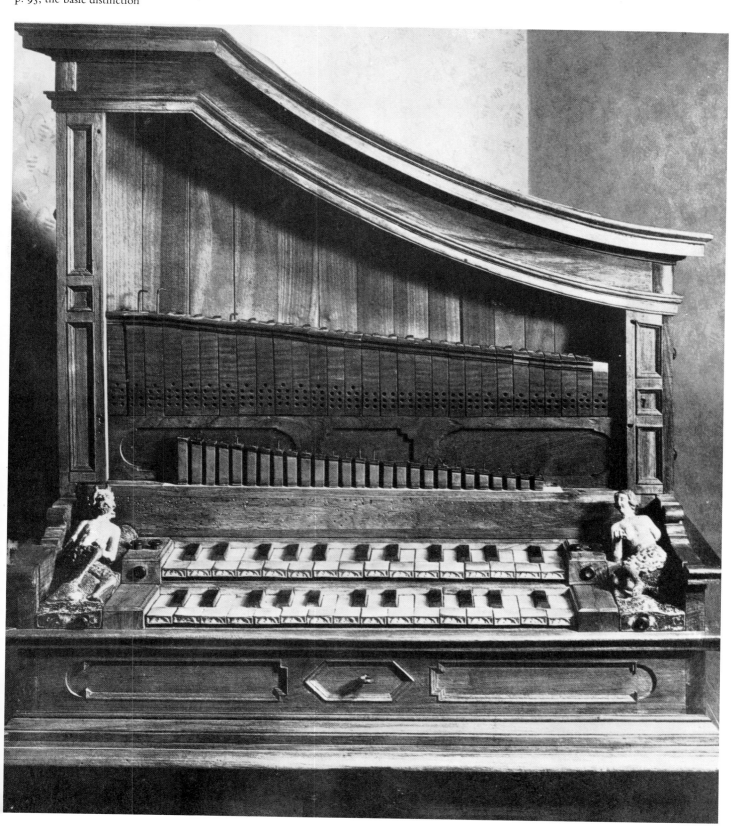

171

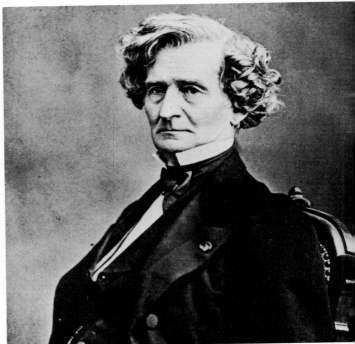

A free reed mouthorgan from Bonanni's *Gabinetto armonico* (1723), whose sound was produced by both sucking and blowing. Its existence in the Orient probably inspired the experimentation in the West which eventually resulted in the invention of a family of related instruments such as the concertina, accordion, harmonium and harmonica.

Hector Berlioz (1803–69) was a highly original orchestrator, who did much to improve and standarize instruments. His *Traité d'instrumentation et d'orchestration modernes* (1844) was the earliest major work of its kind, and is still relevant. This very practical side of his nature is often forgotten when attention is devoted more to the Romantic associations of his music.

FREE REED KEYBOARD INSTRUMENTS

Harmoniums and Accordions

The harmonium is a free reed keyboard instrument. The principle of the free reed—as distinct from the single or double reed, which are fixed—is that of a simple tongue which vibrates through a slot as the wind is blown or sucked through the slot. The principle was known in China and Japan, where it was used in the mouthorgan, for many centuries before it arrived in Western Europe, late in the eighteenth century. In China it was called cheng, and in Japan sho. The accordion uses the same principle, and was a product of virtually the same period—the early nineteenth century. In fact the accordion is in many respects to the harmonium what the portative organ is to the large organ. The body of the accordion is a bellows, with the reeds in the end, with the keyboard at one end and the stops at the other. Both aspiration (sucking in of wind on the principle of the vacuum cleaner) and expiration (blowing out) are used, and this is in element how the harmonium works. The bellows of the harmonium is naturally much larger than that of the accordion, and is controlled by the player with pedals in the centre of the instrument. The Swell and full organ effects are generally operated by projecting arms which can be pressed outward by the player, to left and to right, with his knees, since he ha to keep pedalling all the time he is playing. Possibly the harmonium would have provided ample scope for the village lady organist who, on being asked whether or not she used the pedals of the pipe organ replied, rather curtly, 'Young man, I am not accustomed to acrobatics at the organ stool'

The exact inventor of the harmonium is not known, but in 1840 Alexandre Debain patented a model in Paris which must have been the culmination of much research, doubtless including the work of others also. Debain certainly improve the potential of the harmonium considerably, introducing stops consisting of individual sets of reeds on the lines of th pipe organ. Then followed the expression stop, which disconnected the mechanism for smoothing out the wind supply, and brought the wind pressure directly from the pedals, so that the player could make crescendo and diminu endo (getting loud and soft) at will. Further improvement affected the prominence which could be given to the tun or the bass, the speed with which the reeds sounded, and th steadiness of the wind pressure. The quality of the free-reed instruments is wavery at the best of times—despite the ease o execution achieved by virtuosi on the mouthorgan and ac cordion, for example—but it is for some reason much mo apparent on the harmonium, especially when the wind suppl

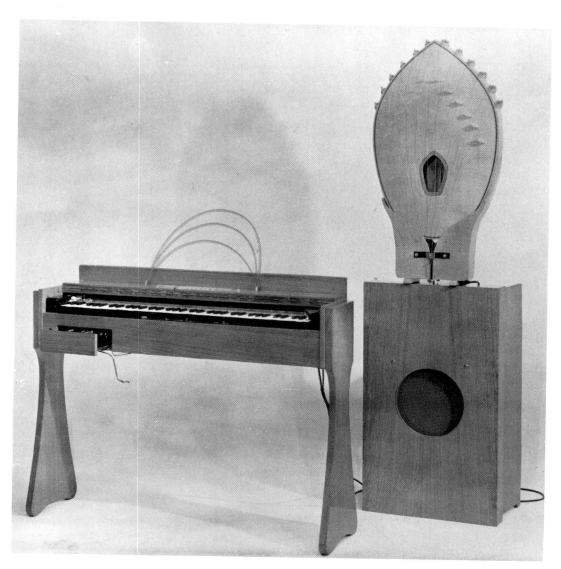

Right: The Ondes Martenot is one of the few new musical instruments of the post-electric era. With its traditional keyboard it is visibly at home among this group of instruments nonetheless.

is breathy. And yet Berlioz, who had a highly acute ear for sonorities, wrote for it as an accompaniment to voices, so one can only assume that the quality of instrument and some of the aspects of technique have been lost. All too often nowadays it conjures up visions of Church Sunday schools, or agonizing attendance at rustic conventicles.

Before leaving the keyboard instruments there is a final group which must be considered. Since a variety of materials is used for the resonating part of the instruments, the basic unifying factor of this group is the striking mechanism.

Glockenspiel

The glockenspiel had various antecedents and counterparts, though there is much to be said for the theory that the earliest developments, in the West at least, were probably inspired by the carillons of the Low Countries, which were so arranged that they could ultimately be played from a keyboard. Obviously they belong as much to the percussion section, since the method of sounding is essentially an action of percussion, and the resonating parts are not characteristic of wind or strings. Also, the keyboard is in fact optional. However, insofar as they influenced certain other instruments, it has been decided to include them at this point. Bach used a

glockenspiel in Cantata 53, *Schlage doch, Gewünschte Stunde*; Handel used one in *Saul* (1738) and Mozart in *The Magic Flute* (1791).

In 1886, a Frenchman, Auguste Mustel, had the idea of placing tuned steel plates over wooden resonators, and incorporated within the framework of a piano, and in so doing invented the celesta. The effect of the resonators is to cut down some of the higher harmonics and so strengthen the fundamental of each note. A subsequent development was the dulcitone, in which the plates were replaced with tuning forks.

Finally, a keyboard instrument which is one of the few products of the post-electric era to have been accepted in the world of classical music from a very early date is the Ondes Martenot. It is an electronic instrument with amplifier, and is played from a keyboard, which explains its inclusion at this point. *Onde* in French means wave, particularly in relation to wavelengths, and it is a good indication of the nature of the instrument. Its implications for the world of musical instruments will be considered more fully in the next chapter. Suffice it to say here that after almost half a century of existence, the Ondes Martenot have failed to make any great impression on music.

Right: Francesco Landini was born in Florence about 1325 and died there in 1397. He was blind from childhood, but was an eminent composer and a virtuoso performer on the portative organ. In fact when he died it was decided that a worthy tribute to him and his talents would be to depict him on his tombstone playing the organ.
Opposite: the Compenius organ at Fredericksborg Castle, Hillerød, Denmark, which dates from the early 17th century. Compenius was a German organ builder, and this particular organ is so important because it has never been altered or tampered with over the years.

Contemporary Instruments

The Future

At the present time, the future of musical instruments seems to offer a variety of possibilities. The classical repertoire will continue to be played, with more and more attention paid to the composer's original intentions. People who are not acquainted with the composer's orchestration or dynamic and metronomic markings may be quite surprised at some of the liberties certain conductors have presumed to take in the interests of 'improved' performances, even when the composer was quite specific as to his intentions, which is not always the case, by any means. The days of the arranger-conductor in the tradition of the late Sir Thomas Beecham are apparently over, at least for the time being. This is not to belittle the magnificent work he and others did in the interests of music, but at present the tide is flowing in the opposite direction.

The traditional instruments of the symphony orchestra as it has evolved to the present time will doubtless continue in use, too, with progressive improvement in the technique of both players and makers. One hesitates to speculate as to the amount of room for improvement left, but bearing in mind that a four-minute mile was once thought unlikely, if not impossible, then it would be unwise to put a limit to man's potential for development in this particular field. Composers will presumably continue to write for the classical orchestra, though obviously exploiting its possibilities to the full as far as technique, timbre, range and physical ability will permit.

It would be unrealistic, however, not to admit that there is a certain area of doubt and dilemma. In the past the resources of the instrument, whether realized or potential, and the talent of the composer have been mutually inspiring. Instruments have improved, in part at least, through the demands composers have made upon them, and composers have produced works which have, from time to time, given the instrumental literature a completely new dimension. When the score of Schubert's Great Symphony was first put before the orchestra it was pronounced impossible to play by the woodwind. However, one finds composers writing now in such a way that the effects the instruments are required to produce are often entirely unrepresentative of their inherent qualities. In a work published in 1963 one reads such instructions to the pianists as: 'improvise on piano strings'; 'rub strings with wire brush' or 'rasp the black keys'. The effect here becomes one of non-melodic percussion, and certainly not that of a specified note at pitch. If, for other parts of its involvement in a work, the piano, or whatever other instrument it may be, is required to be played in more or less the traditional way, then these directions are merely intermittent departures, though of doubtful utility.

It would seem more reasonable, if the composer is going to write frequently and exclusively for the instrument in this way, that either the instrument should be modified, or a new instrument be designed. It would appear a retrograde step, in view of the history of the development of the instrument, and the immense amount of work devoted by the makers of past ages to producing an instrument capable of such tonal subtleties, if it were simply to be treated as a piece of wood.

Doubtless pianos and many other instruments are capable of more subtle effects than we have yet imagined. With the genius of a Berlioz or a Bartok this is conceivable, but one is subjected to a great deal of effects on the lines of 'strike with hammer' in contemporary music. Bartok once directed a cymbal to be scratched on its edge with a penknife—a rather more subtle approach!

New instruments are being developed, though in a somewhat haphazard way at times, one feels. The Frenchman François Baschet has created some instruments which make stunning pieces of modern sculpture with their great wing-like sound deflectors and bristling wires like a series of antennae. One of his first excursions into the realm of making instruments was an inflatable soundbox for his guitar, which he subsequently patented. Some of his later instruments

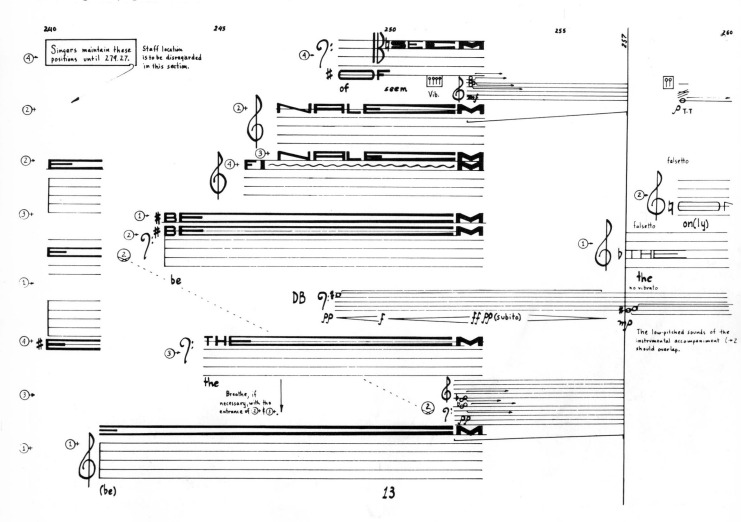

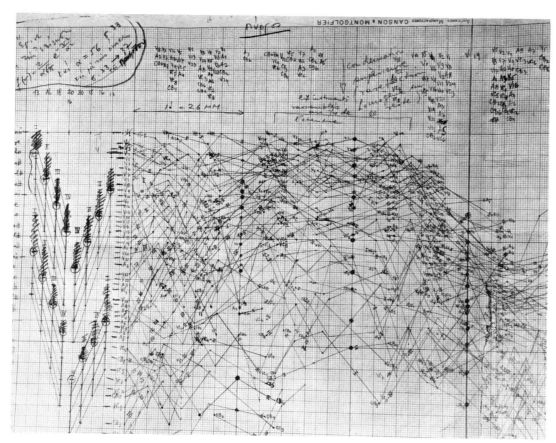

Opposite top: the French composer and conductor Pierre Boulez in front of a caricature of Igor Stravinsky by Jean Cocteau. The relationship of these two very important 20th-century musicians to each other in terms of musical evolution is very striking, and between them they will virtually span the century.

Left: a score by the Greek composer Xenakis, which shows that today much more is being required of instrumentalists than that they should simply be able to play their instruments well. They must also be able to interpret and decipher the composer's instructions and intentions as well.

Below: two pages from The Emperor of Ice Cream by the American composer Roger Reynolds, published in 1963. In the words of the introduction, 'the score dictates not only sounds but also the movements and configuration of singers and instrumentalists on stage. The composition is a chamber work . . .'

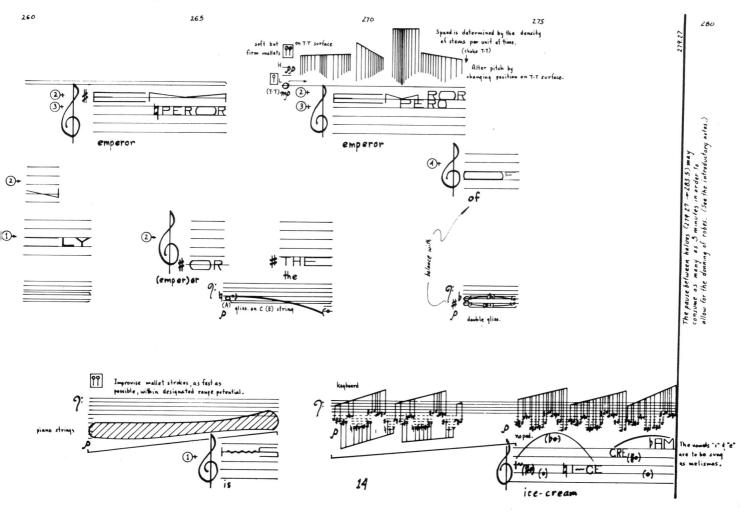

Iannis Xenakis (b.1922), as a young man, was an assistant to the architect Le Corbusier for more than ten years. This doubtless influenced some of his earlier works, which he himself saw as 'aural transliterations of architectural phenomena', and certainly his interest in musical space and textural blocks is the hallmark of his output.

involve rubbing glass tubes with moistened fingers, though the glass harmonica has a prior claim for this particular feature, and large sound deflectors are included in almost all of them –including a small harp.

François Baschet has not yet taken the musical world by storm, and the paths of musical history are strewn with the wrecks of instruments which were to revolutionize music. The Baschet instruments have been found to be excellent for Mozart, which is of no musical interest whatsoever. What is potentially of much greater interest is the fact that the composer Jacques Lasry has written music for them. For these new instruments, or any new instruments for that matter, to be of value there must be composers to exploit their possibilities and performers trained to play them. This is one of the more exciting aspects of the future of musical instruments.

Then of course there is the whole field of electronic music which is, for the most part, completely alien to the development of music over the thousands of years of its history, and therefore requires a totally different set of critical and auditory faculties from those with which we approach classical music. It seems highly unlikely that the majority of 'music lovers' will bridge the gap for some time to come. Indeed it is questionable to what extent traditional forms of creating and writing music will ever be compatible with the world of electronics. We may be in danger of bending over

backwards in attempting to make a synthesis, and it may be more sensible to keep the two apart. There need be nothing despairing about such a counsel.

By way of definition, electronic instruments are those which use electronic means to produce or modify sounds. In practice the term has a very wide application, for the sound of any musical instrument may be picked up by a microphone and subsequently modified by electronic means, and the most frequent use of the term 'electronic' or 'electric' is found in this context. However, since all that is involved is the application of a microphone or electro-magnetic pick-up to the instrument, and passing the sound through an amplifier, 'amplified' would be a perfectly adequate piece of terminology. The 'electric' guitar is perhaps the most common example of this type of instrument, though it is by no means restricted to the world of Pop music. Indeed, for a public clavichord recital, for example, some amplification is almost obligatory if the instrument is to be heard at all.

The concept of amplification is a most important one nevertheless, since it leads on to the introduction of electronic modification. This may only involve volume, but it can also mean the introduction of treble and bass filters for tone control, vibrato and tremolo which can be altered at will, and the ring modulator—and 'fuzz box', as it is commonly known. We shall return to the ring modulator, since it is an

Karlheinz Stockhausen (b.1928) is one of the most respected avant-garde composers of the second half of the 20th century, and certainly possesses one of the most original minds of those working in the field of electronic music. His discriminating taste and ear for sonorities have done much to win more adherents to the cause of contemporary music.

Jean Barraqué (b.1928) was a student of Olivier Messiaen for his analysis classes at the Paris Conservatoire from 1948 to 1951, and spent the next three years in the French Radio's *musique concrète* studio. He is a serial composer in the tradition of Schoenberg rather than Webern, and has been compared to Beethoven on account of his approach to composition.

important element, along with harmonisers, vocoders, parametric equalisers, and other audio signalling processing devices now available, in the work of avant-garde composers at the present time. Before doing so, however, it would be as well to clarify the basic terminology of electronic instruments. There are three very different types of instrument—or machine, since that is effectively what is involved.

The first type consists of those machines that were, from the beginning (and electronic instruments were envisaged in the nineteenth century) created to supplement existing instruments, but which were comparable with those instruments in the way they were to be played, and in the timbre and register they were capable of producing. In this category, only the Ondes Martenot, dating from 1928, can be said to have won a firm place among conventional instruments and in the concert hall.

The second type consists of machines which were intended to copy existing acoustic instruments, not necessarily in every aspect, since it is possible to remove what may be regarded as imperfections in the tonal quality of the acoustic instruments, simplify the way in which they are played, and indeed add features which were not previously present. Here one might mention the electric organ and electric piano.

The third type consists of the various varieties of synthesizer, and it is here that possibly the most exciting developments have taken place. The synthesizer creates and processes sounds by electronic means in real time. In this way all the properties of those sounds—including pitch, volume, timbre and reverberation, for example—may be automatically controlled. More significantly, no doubt, it is possible to build continuous sequences of sound without having to edit tapes, as was necessary previously.

One tends to take the tape recorder very much for granted, but it was only after World War II that it became generally available, and its impact on the development of electronic music should not be underestimated. For instance, a tape recorder permits variations in the playback speed of a tape, thus affecting the frequency and the duration of the recorded sounds. If the speed at which the tape is played back is increased, then the frequency is higher, and the duration is naturally shorter.

Another very important aspect is that any number of sounds can be brought together through the simple means of recording each sound on individual pieces of tape and then splicing them together. Another feature of splicing is that one is able to create a continuous loop of tape, and so produce an ostinato or repeated element. Tapes may also be played in reverse, so that what was once a diminuendo or dying sound is suddenly converted into a crescendo.

These are perhaps rather basic, even crude, operations by present-day standards, but more sophisticated ones were on the way. By recording different elements on parallel tape tracks, it was possible to superimpose them by playing them into a mixer, and then re-recording the resultant effect on to another tape. Furthermore, once one had a definitive tape, as far as the recorded elements were concerned, it could be then subjected to the additional electronic modifications already mentioned, such as filters, reverberation and modulation control, etc.

In the wake of the tape recorder, the development of the synthesizer greatly extended the facilities available to exponents of electronic music. Most synthesizers are in fact made up of individual elements or 'modules', capable of being put together in a variety of ways. In most of them their devices may be controlled individually by external voltages, so that it is not necessary for the operator to intervene to vary volume and sound characteristics. The sheer variety of the sounds that may be produced by a synthesizer is remarkable, and is far greater than that of a mechanical instrument, though at the same time they resemble the sounds produced by conventional instruments rather than those of nature, for example, or the spoken word.

Perhaps the most appealing feature of the synthesizer for the composer interested in electronic music is that–unlike most other methods of electronic sound synthesis–it is able to produce sound in real time. Thus one finds a composer such as Stockhausen using live electronic techniques combined with both conventional and electronic instruments, along with tape recorders and radio receivers.

Nevertheless most synthesizers have limitations when it comes to producing sound in real time. The limitations are imposed in part by the number and nature of the component elements, but more importantly by the number of operations the executant is capable of carrying out. One may well find that a synthesizer is used to produce only one 'voice' or sound at a time, and these sounds have to be recorded individually and then mixed. In view of this drawback as far as live performance is concerned, some synthesizers have been created specifically with live performance in mind.

For live performance is still of paramount importance for a composer such as Stockhausen, even when electronically produced music plays such an important part in his *oeuvre*. In his *Mixtur* (1964), the sounds from five different instrumental groups are picked up by microphones and fed into the same number of ring modulators, each one controlled individually. The modified sounds are then broadcast through five loudspeakers and blended with live orchestral sounds. A similar process is used in *Mantra* (1970), using two pianos and two ring modulators whereas in *Telemusik* (1966) and *Hymen* (1967) ring modulators are introduced into what are basically tape compositions.

The ring modulator takes its name from the way in which four diodes are arranged in its circuit, and in an electronic studio it is capable of producing totally new and complex mixtures of sound. Alternatively, it may be used to transform

existing material. One example of the sort of effect that may be achieved is that produced when the frequency of the input signal is varied, and the result is a multiple glissando effect. In the division of electronic instruments into the two categories of sound generators and sound modifiers, however, the ring modulator is essentially a sound modifier.

The rapid development of computer techniques is helping considerably in the field of sound synthesis, as well as in the basic process of composition, for some composers. Computers are now used to control the generation of sound and the equipment used to process it, much as synthesizers do. In fact a computer program can simulate synthesizer devices, though the music it produces cannot be altered in real time. A sound wave may be constructed in digital form, which can be converted into sound with the help of a digital-to-analog convertor. The sound produced in this way can range from an individual tone to a complete composition, and it is therefore evident that it is one of the most versatile means of generating sound. The sound wave is created directly, and there are virtually no limitations on the sounds which may be produced. Moreover, some digital signal processing devices operating under a computer program are now capable of altering sounds in real time.

If it is large enough, virtually any general-purpose computer may be used to generate sound. A composition may be encoded as input, then run on to the computer, and lastly converted into sound. Naturally the fact that there are three processes involved means that there is a certain amount of time lag from the moment of conception to the act of realization, but even so, the composer and his audience will probably hear the work sooner than they would if it were a question of an instrumental piece. Some home computers now have specially designed sound chips which are able to

The explosion that occurred in the realm of pop music after World War II gave enormous impetus to the involvement of young people in performing that music, especially via the guitar in the early days. Certainly many more people became involved in the making of live music than might otherwise have been the case. Seen here is the group Orchestral Manoeuvres in the Dark. What is somewhat regrettable, however, is the high degree of commercial exploitation of this phenomenon, with its seemingly insatiable demand for novelty and stimulation, which has tended to put musical considerations rather lower on the list of priorities than one would have hoped for in such an implicitly important part of Western culture.

produce sound instantaneously from a user-prepared program. Despite these developments– and there have been others not detailed here, such as the use of silver electrodes picking up alpha-waves from the brain of the performer – there are still technical problems to overcome, and in certain areas there will undoubtedly be developments with consequences as yet unforeseen. The hope of the average music-lover, however, must be that the whole realm of electronic music will come to be guided more by purely musical considerations than it seems to be at present. Indeed, it could well be argued that the world of Pop music has been much more prepared to embrace the possibilities offered by electronics, than has the mainstream of Classical music.

Somewhat paradoxically, perhaps, as electronic means of generating sounds have proliferated, we have witnessed an extraordinary revival of interest in hearing old music performed on the instruments for which it was written, or on faithful modern reproductions. More than that, it seems that what we are tending to witness at the present time is a growing belief that pre-Classical music must only be heard on authentic instruments. The fatal flaw in such an approach is that, try as we might, we can no longer listen with pre-Classical ears and minds. Surely the eventual conclusion reached must be that to use only authentic instruments for pre-Classical music is as extreme a doctrine as never to use them at all.

But the whole question of revivals and reproductions creates problems and splits the musical camp into factions. How far is one to go in the utilization of authentic materials, and to what extent should modern ones be substituted? The argument that the composer might have preferred such a sound and the instrument makers might have used certain materials, had they been available, is only partly admissible. More cogent is the argument that the composers wrote with certain sounds in mind and we can only have a certain amount of insight into their intentions. This goes for many aspects of the performance of music by pre-Romantic composers when we try to get as near as possible to the timbre they heard in their musical ear as they wrote. Would Beethoven have written some of the chords he did in his piano music if he had at his disposal a fully developed grand piano? Or what might he have written instead? Most of the time we reach a compromise, for the second question is unanswerable, and the first is only of academic interest for most people.

As a general principle, however, most musicians would probably agree that modern synthetic materials should and may be used when they do not substantially alter the essential character of an instrument – whether in restoration or building reproduction instruments – insofar as we are able to determine what the tonal quality of the instrument in question originally was. The question is a very vexed one, and one must be wary of being too dogmatic, for many reproduction instruments merit attention in their own right. The fact that concert halls are today regularly full for programmes of medieval music is an immense tribute to the patience, devotion and persistence of a few pioneers. But although the realm of musical experience in general and the world of musical instruments in particular is enriched, it is hard to see what will have been contributed to the development of the instruments themselves. Being able to hear them is in itself a revelation, and will help us to reappraise the instruments which now constitute the classical orchestra. However, the very fact that instruments have had to be rescued from oblivion shows that they were outside the mainstream. Still, this is the age in which the mainstream has apparently either dried up or gone underground. We can only hope that the incredible ability of musical instruments to adapt, or simply to survive, will see their continuation in the decades ahead.

Perhaps the last words can be left to John Dowland, who has left us some exquisite songs and instrumental music, and yet in his day was known primarily as a lutenist, and was probably the finest exponent in Europe at the time – in rather the same way as Bach was known in his own day much more for his abilities as an organist than as a composer. Dowland was appointed lutenist to the King of Denmark in 1598 at the age of thirty-five, and seemed all set for a glorious career. However, on failing to return from a trip to England, he was dismissed in 1606. He saw his career in ruins, and the very existence of the lute threatened. In fact he was appointed lutenist to King James of England in 1616, so on that score he made a comeback. As to the supremacy of the lute, however, the writing really was on the wall. It survived for another century, but in an increasingly diminished role. The preface to Dowland's *Fourth Book of Airs* is consequently a very interesting document. It was published in 1612, before Dowland returned to the limelight, and is a touching piece of writing. Beneath its quaint turns of phrase it is intensely human, revealing the wounded pride, possibly vanity, of a man who has known better times and who sticks out for his artistic integrity. Dowland had even been prepared to go back to Protestantism (he was a Catholic convert) for his music. 'Worthy Gentlemen, and my loving Countrymen . . . I have lien long obscured from your sight, because I received a Kingly entertainment in a forraine climate [his term of office in Denmark], which could not attaine to any (though never so meane) place at home, yet have I held up my head within this Horizon, and not altogether beene unaffected else where . . . yet I must tell you, as I have beene a stranger; so have I againe found strange entertainement since my return: especially by the opposition of two sorts of people that shroude themselves under the title of Musitians. The first are some simple Cantors, or vocall singers, who though they seeme excellent in their blinde Division-making, are meerely

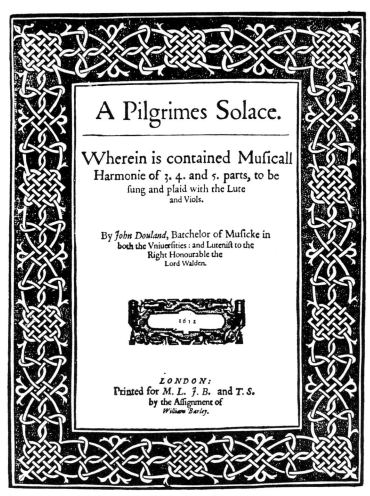

A Pilgrimes Solace.

Wherein is contained Musicall
Harmonie of 3. 4. and 5. parts, to be
sung and plaid with the Lute
and Viols.

By *John Douland*, Batchelor of Musicke in
both the Vniuersities: and Lutenist to the
Right Honourable the
Lord Walden.

1612

LONDON:
Printed for *M. L. J. B.* and *T. S.*
by the Assignment of
William Barley.

ignorant . . . The second are young-men, professors of the Lute, who vaunt themselves, to the disparagement of such as have beene before their time (wherein I myself am a party) that there never was the like of them.'

Dowland goes on to say that instead of praising their own skill, these 'young-men' should be looking to their laurels, because the viol da gamba is stealing the limelight from the lute. It is their business, says Dowland, to refute this new heresy:
'Perhaps you will aske me, why I that have travailed in many countries, and ought to have some experience, doth not under goe this busines my selfe? I answere that I want abilitie, being [sic] I have now entered into the fiftieth yeare of mine age: secondly because I want both meanes, leasure, and encouragement'.

Without making any bones about it he concludes 'abruptly' – to use his own word – and makes it quite clear that he needs an appointment, money and encouragement. Three hundred-and-fifty years later, the cry is still the same. The life of the professional instrumentalist is still as hard as ever. And Dowland was a virtuoso. For every soloist who stands in front of an orchestra today there are a hundred rank-and-file musicians on the platform behind him, possibly no less dedicated to their instrument. The problem is essentially a human one. The world of musical instruments is as much the world of men themselves today as it was thousands of years ago in the age of myth and ritual.

INDEX

ACKNOWLEDGMENTS

Author: 28 L.R.; 118 B; 125. Miss Olive Lloyd-Baker Collection: *14*. Clive Barda: 66–67; 90. Bayerisches Nationalmuseum, Munich: 50 R. Boosey & Hawkes Ltd., London: 52–53 T.B; 55 R; 57 TL; 58–59; 62–63 T; 73 TC; 86. BBC Copyright Photographs: 44–45; 116–117. British Museum, London: 13; 22 T.B; 23; 27; *39 L*; 40 TL.TR; 41 T; 61 T; 74–75; 77; 79; 80; 95. Master & Fellows of Corpus Christi College, Cambridge: 50 L. Country Life: 4. Giraudon, Paris: *93*; *114*. Hamlyn Group Library: 2; *14*; 16 B; *38 B*; *39 R*; 41 B; *42*; *46 T.BL*; 47, 51, 62 L; *81*; 85, 87 T; *92 T.B; Front jacket TR*. Michael Holford Library, London: *39 L*. Imperial Storehouse Shosoin Nara: *Front jacket TR*. Librairie Larousse, Paris: 16 TR; 36 T; *38 T*; 48; 49; 55 LC; 57 B.R; 61–63 B; 65; 69; 70; 71; 72; 73 B; 76; 83; 87; 104 T; 109 T, B; 113; 120 TL; 121 R. London Features International: P. Cox *123*; M. Putland *122*. *Front jacket BR*. Mansell Collection, London: 1; 6–7; 8 T; 18–19; 31. Mansell-Alinari: 68. Mansell-Giraudon: 37. Robert Morley & Co. Ltd., London: 121 R; 124. Peters Editions Ltd., London: 119 B. R.M. Photographic Ltd., London: *123*. Picturepoint Ltd., London: *122*. Réalités, Paris: 118 T; 119 T. Scala, Florence: *10 T.B; 11; 15 T.B.*; 32; *34 L (front jacket BL)*; *35 T.B (front jacket TL)*; *46 BR*; 60; 82; *84*. Steinway & Sons, London: 107. Spurgeon Collection, Greenwich Borough Library: 17. Victoria & Albert Museum, London: 9 B; 12; 26; 29; 56; 64; *81*; *92 B*; 98 T.B; 99 T.B; 100 T.B; 104 B; 106. Roger Viollet, Paris; 36 B. Weidenfeld & Nicolson, London: 78; 111.

Photographs of Emil Gilels and Ralph Kirkpatrick appear by kind permission of Deutsche Grammophon.

The photograph of James Galway appears by kind permission of RCA Limited.

Those numbers printed in italics refer to colour plages.
The sources of some illustrations do not appear in the acknowledgments; these can be found in the captions.

AUTHOR'S NOTE

I should like to express my thanks to Mr Peter Tranchell for the encouragement given in the initial stages of this book's existence, to the staff of the Pendlebury Library in Cambridge for their kindness and understanding, and to Mr Tom Graves for his perseverance in tracking down the illustrations.

I must also thank Mr Benjamin Britten for his generous permission to quote from his programme notes to *Curlew River*.